THE CONSULTANT'S
PLAYBOOK

SHARPEN YOUR CONSULTING SKILLS AND
MAKE A REAL IMPACT WITH YOUR CLIENT

THE CONSULTANT'S PLAYBOOK

SHARPEN YOUR CONSULTING SKILLS AND MAKE A REAL IMPACT WITH YOUR CLIENT

Dan Minkin

CONTENTS

FIGURES

ACKNOWLEDGEMENTS

In the three years since the inception of this book, many people have provided encouragement and guidance.

Of course, my wife, Natalie Minkin, and sons, Matthew and Benjamin. Natalie provided support, encouragement and reviewing expertise, as did Matthew and Benjamin.

My father, Lewis Minkin, who passed away in 2021, is my inspiration for completing this book. He was a scholar and author of significant analyses of the British Labour Movement.

My UK family – mother Lillie Plews, stepmother Liz Minkin, Tom and Stella St David-Smith, and finally, my wife's parents, Peter and Beverley Booker, have all provided love, support, guidance, and a shoulder to cry on over the years.

Other people have contributed massively to my growth over 26 years in IT and consulting. People who have affected my life include Liz Taylor and Tony Roberts, my first mentors of substance at the Co-operative Insurance Society in Manchester; Tim Arnfield, who stopped me from trying to save the world; Mark Blake, who had confidence in me and gave me confidence; Graham Smith, whose intelligent thoughtfulness provided a role model; and Simon Farrant, who allowed me the opportunity to move to a new life and facilitated the trajectory I am on.

Lately, I have relied on and taken guidance from colleagues at Planit Software Testing – Mike Weale, Emma Pilcher, and Jaime Taylor. All have provided guidance of one type or another to give me confidence in what I can do and to improve myself. Also, Deepak Pratap, a friend who has provided some alternative views on professional and career matters.

And finally, those who answered the call to help and in doing so, made me accountable to get this book finished! These people include Ganapathy Iyer, Raewyn Ludlam, Neil Thompson, and Neil Newman.

Thank you to all of you.

INTRODUCTION

As a career consultant, you have a lot of ground to cover. Over time, you may work with hundreds of organisations, thousands of individuals, and across multiple industries. You need to work both in the business, delivering to clients, and on the business, ensuring that you remain up to date, sufficiently well known, and financially successful enough to meet your goals.

That is where *The Consultant's Playbook* comes in. It is your go-to source for how-to activities. It includes processes, activities, guidelines, and checklists. It advises you on actions that are appropriate for a given situation or scenario, and it answers the question "What do I do when ..." across the entire consultant lifecycle.

My goal for this book is to allow professional consultants to make a difference for themselves, for their clients, and for their business, by providing the tools they need. You might be an aspiring partner who needs to understand clients and customer requirements better because your business depends on it. Or you might be an internal consultant, providing advice and guidance for members of your own company.

By investing in *The Consultant's Playbook*, you will be able to:

- Successfully deliver on your engagements more of the time.
- Grow your reputation through improved successful delivery.
- Add real value to your engagements and for your clients.

This book is therefore aimed at:

- Professional consultants who are involved across the lifecycle, either on their own or within a larger organisation, aiming to make a real difference in their impact through continuous improvement activities.

- Consultancy leaders and owners of small and medium-sized consultancy firms, who operate both on the business and in the business, looking for scalability, repeatability, and consistency in their team.

- Junior or less experienced consultants who, as they grow their career, will find that more and more resonates and can be applied.

Whoever you are and whatever you do, I hope you find something of use within the covers of this book.

A Note on Content and Style

This is not a quick-fix book. There are many other books out there that promise to deliver you a seven- or eight-figure income, and there is something to be said for books or methods that have a singular motivational message. I have never found those types of book as satisfying as others, preferring books that I would return to over the years because of their depth and complexity.

Consequently, I have not written the kind of book that contains a 'secret method'. Instead, I wanted to create a framework on which more and more could be built. If a new process would be useful, then it could be added. If another technique that is being used delivers positive results, then that could be added, too. My thinking was that if the framework is clear and complete, then adding additional information would be easy in the future. The style of writing is designed to be thorough and educational rather than familiar because I feel it suits this type of content. It is also the type of book I would want to read. Hopefully, it matches what you want, too.

What's Ahead

Figure 1.   The Consultant's Playbook Structure – High Level

The Consultant's Playbook is divided into five parts. Each of these is covered in an individual chapter.

Chapter 1 – Activate, covers the fundamentals of your role as a consultant, the capability you need to deliver, the services you provide and the clients you will meet. Your strategy needs to bring these elements together so that you have a plan for your future.

Chapter 2 – Acquire, discusses the process of articulating your offering during sales and contracting activities. The objective of the activities in this chapter is to win business so that you can provide your services to clients.

Chapter 3 – Advise, explores the process of analysing client requirements and designing and validating solutions. This is the chapter that covers what most people would think of as archetypical consulting activities.

Chapter 4 – Act, is about taking the outputs and decisions made during the Advise process and delivering outcomes to the client that result in meaningful and valuable change for them. This is done through well-managed initiation, delivery, and end phases.

Chapter 5 – Abilities, covers the personal and soft skills you need as a consultant to perform across the wide range of activities and situations that consultancy brings about.

Throughout the book are the **four key practices** of **Marketing, Adding Value, Customer Service,** and **Knowledge Management**. While they are introduced at various points in the book, they are relevant to *all* points in the lifecycle, and you should strive for them to become second nature to you.

Chapter 1 – Activate

Activate involves putting in place the necessary foundations to provide successful consulting deliveries. You need to understand the elements that make a successful consultant *before* you have the opportunity to perform any consultancy.

Consultants come in varieties. You can be a facilitator, working to extract solutions from clients, or you can be an expert, trading on your knowledge and deep experience of your topic. You may prefer to work internally, embedded in an organisation in a permanent capacity; or externally, as a fully independent operator. And there are a number of company structures that might support you in your career, ranging from solo operator to multi-national advisory and consultancy companies. By considering these environmental factors, you can find your most effective positioning and set yourself up as an adaptable individual who acts the right way in any situation.

Your **Capability** is what you have the ability to do. You need to consider how to continually develop personally – for your benefit and that of your clients. You must strive to assess how your capability matches the client and market need. Finally, you need to continually demonstrate your capability so that your clients have a real feel for what you do and how you can help them.

Your **Services** are what you deliver as a consultant. A client will engage with you because they have a need. As a consultant, you will engage them because you provide a service which matches that need and, typically, because the client has a shortage of such skills in-house. But what is the best way to define what you do and what services you provide? By function, by domain, by delivery method, by intellectual property (IP)? These are all valid ways of doing it, but whatever you decide, relevance and consistency are key.

The next focus is the **Client**. The client is the consultant's customer, and without the client, there would be no consultancy! This interaction is fundamental but varies between situations in the types of clients you interact with, the closeness to each one, their specific motivations and fears, and the importance that both of you attach to the relationship.

The last Activate step is **Strategy**. Your strategy is what brings the consulting, capability, services, and client elements together. In addition, you need to consider fundamental aspects of how you wish to perform your consultancy activities, including your purpose (also known as your mission), your values, and your vision for the future. You may also need to consider more detailed planning, such as roadmaps and targets. Finally, you need to consider how you communicate your strategy to potential clients and colleagues.

Additionally, the first **key practice** is introduced. **Marketing** is about proactively promoting yourself, your services, and your capability. It provides a valuable avenue for generating business, particularly so for trying to break into new domains or sectors where relationships do not exist, and reputation has not yet been established. Marketing provides a number of clear benefits, but the type of marketing that you do and when you do it will be situation and context dependent.

Chapter 2 – Acquire

Chapter 2, Acquire, covers the period where the two parties involved in the consulting relationship – you as the consultant, and the client – make themselves visible to each other and agree to do business together. This stage is marked by a gradual coming together over time, with a final stage of being tied into a mutually beneficial arrangement by formally making an agreement. Sales and Contracting are the key steps in the Acquire stage.

Sales is the act of making contact and communicating with potential clients so that they might consider doing business with you. In larger organisations, this may be performed by a separate sales or account function. In smaller organisations, it is often performed by the same individual who performs the engagement itself. Either way, selling and consulting are almost inseparable.

Contracting is an iterative step, performed every time a new piece of work is agreed in principle. The purpose of contracting is threefold: to unambiguously detail the agreement between the parties while setting precedent for the working arrangements; to confirm the agreement to proceed; and to provide a risk-reduction mechanism for both parties through contractually enforceable means.

Chapter 3 – Advise

This chapter covers the Advise stage, which is the consulting lifecycle. It includes the activities and steps that consultants perform every time they engage with a client. The process is complete and comprehensive but also flexible – not every step is performed every time.

The Advise stage begins with the **Analyse** step. Here you begin with the need, requirement, or problem you received from the client, and which was explored in the Sales step of the Acquire stage. This requirement can be well defined, clear, and complete. It may also be poorly defined, unclear, or incomplete. Once you have the requirement, you will need to make further queries to define what it is that the client wishes to achieve and, therefore, what the "true need" is.

Next is the **Design** step. When you have captured sufficient information and built up enough knowledge of the situation, a likely range of solutions will present themselves. There may be an early favourite for you at this time. Options should be determined to ensure that the client and not you, the consultant, decides what is best for their circumstances.

The final step is **Validate**. At this third step you go through the process of outlining the options, and the pros and cons of each, and then make a recommendation. In some cases, a recommendation becomes a proposal and then a contract. This part of the stage is marked by an iterative process of documenting solutions, presenting, and amending, which continues until the recommendation is accepted or you agree to go no further with the client.

The second **key practice, Adding Value,** is covered here. Adding Value is important because consultancy is fundamentally a value-based activity. A client expects value in return for payment, usually a greater value than the initial outlay. So, as a consultant, you have to sell the value of your offering. That is, explain and reinforce the reasons why your services and solutions are valuable to the client and why they should choose you rather than another consultant. If you are unable to do so, then why would any client want to work with you or pay a price that you believe is fair? You will find it useful to understand how the focus on value accumulates, and how to consider it from both a quantitative and a qualitative perspective.

Chapter 4 - Act

Act is all about delivery. Not all engagements go further than the Advise stage, but for those that do, in order to be successful, it is recommended that there be three well-managed steps: Initiation, Delivery, and Ending. This chapter discusses the process of taking the recommendations from the Advise stage and putting them into practice through delivery.

The **Initiate** step sets the mood for the rest of the engagement. Clients are looking for an early signal that the consultant can deliver, so you need to hit the ground running whilst at the same time performing in a way that is sustainable and honest. This is the time to focus on understanding culture and stakeholders, and to ensure that the conditions for the rest of the engagement are being set up. Now is also the time to perform any clarification that may be needed. Finally, you should consider what key performance indicators (KPIs) to use to measure the success of the engagement.

The second step, **Solutions Delivery,** is the key to both a successful engagement and a happy client. It is the combination of skills, knowledge, and experience that you bring, which builds into an effective delivery. In addition, you may now have a role in managing and controlling the service delivery as well as providing any necessary governance. You will also need to navigate through troubled waters from time to time, managing difficult situations and avoiding dangerous ones that could jeopardise the client's success or your own.

The **End** of an assignment has a significant effect on the perception of success. To leave a good impression, you must ensure that the delivery has been accepted and that you have made good on all promises. You should be clear on the value that has been added by the engagement and that success has been measured against the KPIs set up in the initial part of the engagement. Finally, you will look to the future, planning for your next engagement, either with the existing client or with new ones.

The third **key practice** is **Customer Service**. Good customer service comes from thoroughly understanding your customer's desires, fears, and hopes, and responding in a way which demonstrates that the client comes first. Great customer service comes from going above and beyond in ways that cannot go unnoticed.

Chapter 5 – Abilities

Whilst you need expert skills, you also need to develop a range of personal skills if you want to succeed in consultancy. These "soft skills" are a fundamental part of the playbook of the consultant, and you will find yourself using a wide range of them over any given assignment. Whilst you do not need to be exceptional across the board, it is important that you work to reduce any weaknesses until they are no longer liabilities.

"Soft skills" can be grouped into the following broad categories:

- **Communication** skills, that is, speaking, listening, writing, and presenting.

- **Problem-Solving** skills, using different types of thinking.

- **Self-Management** skills to keep yourself motivated, confident, and productive.

- **Working with Others**, including teamwork and influence.

The final **key practice** is **Knowledge Management**. The ability to learn from each engagement is important to consultants and consultancies. It is the fact that consultants can claim to have some experience in having done something before that makes them valuable to clients. Without this, consultants have little to offer other than being an extra pair of hands. In addition, consultants strive to leave clients more educated than when they arrive.

1
ACTIVATE

Figure 2.   The Consultant's Playbook Structure – Activate Steps and Activities

In this chapter you will learn which activities will help you position your-self as a consultant. You will learn about the various types of consultant and how to define your Services and to understand your Client. You will also discover how to develop the right Capability to meet the market need. You will also see how the Strategy brings this together so you can implement a successful consulting business. The first key practice, Marketing, is explained.

Consultant

A consultant is an individual who adapts to perform multiple roles, using their knowledge and skills to influence or deliver beneficial change on behalf of a client. This is a broad definition. Within it, a consultant is not restricted to having to perform specific or narrow actions, but instead has the right to define their role as they see fit. Consultancy has an equally broad definition. We can define it as the activity of using knowledge and skills to advise and help, in order to deliver beneficial change to a client.

Both definitions are purposefully wide because they cover an extremely varied set of real-world activities.

In fact, consulting is a hugely broad profession, covering activities from providing an hour's advice to multi-year and multi-million dollar engagements, from providing an extra pair of hands to taking responsibility for organisational change, and from working as a single and independent expert to being part of a multi-national management consulting firm. Consultants can play many roles in many ways to achieve the outcome they seek. It is important that you understand this innate variety of consultancy roles. It sets the foundations for your effectiveness as a consultant for the following reasons:

- First, it allows you to recognise what type of consultant you are and, therefore, be able to more accurately describe this to clients. This then allows you to focus on your strengths, to leverage your skills and perform other actions that build on your current competencies. In doing so, you increase your credibility.

- Second, it promotes a mindset of adaptability, the drive to find other ways of doing things. It encourages you to approach problems in different ways than you might otherwise do. It sets you up to try new ways of working.

- Third, it helps you frame an important message to your clients – that consultants come in many valid shapes and sizes. If your clients understand all the ways in which you can help, it may open other opportunities for you, growing your profile and ultimately increasing your success as a consultant.

The Five Elements Common to all Consulting Engagements

Although consultancy is a wide-ranging discipline, there are common themes that run through the profession, which draw together the disparate activities performed.

The following five elements are common across all consulting engagements. Consultants always:

- **Advise.** They provide advice based on their skills and experience in areas of expertise, which the other party typically does not have.

- **Augment.** They fill a gap where companies have a lack of appropriately skilled resources.

- **Add value.** They can add both tangible and intangible value to the client because they have the skills and knowledge required to meet the client's requirements, and they are able to impart this through knowledge transfer or delivery activities.

- **Facilitate change.** They add value in a major way through influencing activities that result in organisational change.

- **Leave.** They are only there temporarily as companies often have requirements that need to be satisfied in a defined timeframe. The impact of the engagement, though, and the relationship, will hopefully be much longer lasting.

Even though these are the common themes, they are not all equally weighted at all times. At any given point in the consultant lifecycle, one or another could be at the forefront and the others in the background. Consultants need to adapt by focusing clearly on the purpose that best fits the situation there and then.

Whilst there are common themes in consultancy, equally there are significant variations in how it is performed. To fully understand these differences, to understand the variety of consultancy, you need to look at consultancy from several perspectives: the core capability, the position of the consultant, the roles that are played, the employment structure of the consultant, and the amount of leverage used.

Perspective 1 – Core Capability

In your professional capacity you will need to develop a range of skills and specialist knowledge that allows you to share this expertise effectively and efficiently. Broadly speaking, your career will take you down one of two core capability paths: Expert Consultancy or Process Consultancy.

Expert Consultancy

Consultants are experts and must be perceived as such. As an expert in your field, you trade on your expertise achieved through gathering more and more experience performing similar activities across multiple engagements. This allows you to generate consultant-led solutions, taking the client along with you to an outcome that delivers value and a return on investment for your time.

Your expertise is a function of five elements:

- **Capability.** Capability is what you have the skills to do, including your areas of expertise and domains of knowledge. Your capability is a factor of your own actions, now and in the past.

- **Credentials.** Your credentials are your suitability to take on a particular task, as demonstrated by previous experience and achievements. Your credentials are a factor of your capability, plus the proof of that capability. Your credentials are your track record.

- **Capacity.** Your capacity is the ability to produce what is needed at the time it is needed. This is usually a factor of your bandwidth and the availability of any other tools or support you need.

- **Qualifications.** Your qualifications are your formal records of training you have completed, examinations you have passed, and accreditations you have received. They are certifications by external bodies attesting that you have achieved a certain level of competence and expertise in a subject area.

- **Reputation.** Your reputation is the external perception of your ability to provide a quality service based on all the previous factors but, in particular, your credentials.

4

Process Consultancy

Consultants have another core capability and potential career path. As a process consultant, rather than delivery of expertise, you use a range of process and facilitation techniques to extract data and knowledge from a client, leading them towards their own options and solution. These client-led solutions contrast with the consultant-led solutions of expert consultancy.

The Three Key Skills of a Process Consultant

Skill	Description
Problem Solving	In this role you define and manage a problem-solving process. Your aim is to give clients a structure to achieve their own solutions and objectives. This type of consultancy can lead to very high buy-in situations as well as greater effectiveness because of the greater input from individuals who know their business well.
Collaboration	Because process consulting involves a great deal of collaboration, you need to develop a range of skills to support this activity, such as facilitation, coaching, and conflict resolution. Your negotiation and communication skills will need to be strong, as will your emotional intelligence.
Organisational	The final category of skills you need are organisational. This means developing an understanding of group dynamics, leadership and management styles, and organisational behaviour as well as the techniques and tools to implement appropriate strategies.

Process consulting can be the method used for an entire engagement, or it can be one technique used by expert consultants. The appropriateness of this depend on client culture, client expectations, and the amount of time available to deliver value.

Perspective 2 – Consultant Position

While most consultants are external to the organisation they work in, this is not always the case. As a consultant, you can be external or internal.

Whether you are an external consultant bringing technical expertise, or internal bringing company knowledge, you still aim to deliver independent advice for the benefit of your client.

- **External consultants.** You are external to the organisation in which you deliver services and typically take defined, short-term roles with a defined target outcome. You bring skills and experience that are not internally available to the client, and it is these credentials that make you attractive. The engagement process can be quite lengthy and complex, with the full consultant lifecycle from the start of the sales activities to the end of the delivery engagement, all wrapped up with what could be extensive commercial and legal activities.

  Your outsider status means that significant work has to be put into building relationships and developing trust, as well as establishing frameworks for the engagement, even though these frameworks are temporary. Whilst you have experience as an external consultant, you have little or no direct power to make changes. Instead, you rely on your communication and influencing skills, and on tactics developed from your experience of successful change management.

- **Internal consultants.** In this situation, you are directly employed by the organisation in which you work, to advise and consult, usually on a specific and focused area. You may be part of a small team of internal consultants, and unless your team has budget to expand, your resources are finite because of this size. You will likely have a deeper understanding of the internal organisation and its strategy and culture than an external consultant will. However, you are not truly independent and are potentially more vulnerable to the internal politics and pressures that exist.

  Your internal status means less work is required to engage with the internal client (no contracts or legal documents, though there may be terms of references that define the engagement), and because you are there for the long term, you will likely need to spend less time developing trust or demonstrating your credentials as these are already established.

Perspective 3 – The Roles that are Played

Figure 3. Spectrum of Roles Played by Consultants

At different times and in different environments, the same consultant needs to perform different roles for the good of their client. Sometimes this is several roles at once. The most successful consultants can adapt their behaviour to what the situation demands at that precise time.

It may help to visualise these roles across a spectrum from one extreme point on a scale, where the emphasis is on the client to be the active party in the engagement (consultant as Supporter), to the other, where the consultant is the key driver (consultant as Leader).

Consultant Roles

Skill	Description
Supporter	A consultant can act as a supporter, providing encouragement, confidence, and a sense of validation to the client.
Coach	As a coach, through questioning and challenging, the consultant takes a more active role to help the client create and subsequently deliver their own solutions.
Expert	As an expert, the consultant starts to become more prominent and has the chance to start influencing and persuading to achieve organisational change.
Change Seed	As a change seed, the role becomes more explicit, and the client will sponsor or direct the consultant to perform activities that are designed to accelerate change.
Pair of Hands	As a pair of hands, the consultant takes an active role in creating the solution and is a fully integrated part of the project or change team.

Skill	Description
Leader	As a leader, the consultant becomes as close to acting as a client manager as is possible, taking responsibility from the client for the delivery and successful outcomes. It is, however, unusual for a consultant to take this role and consideration is required before assuming such responsibility.

Perspective 4 – Employment Structure

There are several different organisational structures that you might work under. Each differs in terms of the responsibility, range of assignments, and the opportunity for growth they may afford you as a consultant. At any given time, you may decide that one structure is better than another for your career, and over time, you may experience employment under each of the various structures.

Consultant Employment Structures

Structure	Description
Sole Consultant	Freedom to take what work you want, and to work how you want, are the major upsides of a solo consultancy. This is what drives many people to become an independent entity. The risks include variable income (potentially very high), and the need to find your own work. Sole consultants sometimes find the sales aspect of the role challenging.
Partner/Co-owner	If you are one of a small number of partners (co-owners) in an organisation, you will benefit from a larger and more flexible structure to sell, support, and deliver work. There may, however, be reduced opportunity to choose what type of work, and how much of it, to deliver as the realities of working in a more commercially-focused entity hit home.

Structure	Description
Small (Boutique) Consultancy	This organisation will provide support and possibly a more effective sales operation. In addition, if the consultancy has a niche that matches your specialism, then this may be a perfect fit. Small consultancies, though, can provide limited variety, and often find themselves under considerable commercial pressure with the ebbs and flows of work that consultancy generates. There are tens of thousands of these types of organisations providing consultancy or other professional services across the world, from legal firms to human resources service providers.
Research and Advisory	Included in this category are organisations such as Gartner, Nielsen, and Ovum. These organisations focus on knowledge acquisition and distillation, and often specialise in a certain domain, such as technology or marketing. These firms are often approached when organisations are looking to find the latest trends in the market, or to obtain advice on which other service providers are a suitable match for their requirements. As an advisor in this sort of firm, you will spend large amounts of time researching and meeting with clients who wish to take advantage of your research, analysis, and insights.
Expert Networks	Expert networks pair corporate clients, or investment funds, with individuals in the market who may have access to on-the-ground knowledge about certain industries or geographies. This can often be taken up in addition to engaging with the Research and Advisory sector. This type of consulting is ad hoc and occasional but is potentially lucrative. Companies who provide this type of service are middlemen and include GLG and AlphaSights.
Large (Tier 1 or Tier 2) Consultancy	Large consultancies include McKinsey & Company, Bain & Company, and Boston Consulting Group, each with well over 10,000 employees. Working in these types of large organisation may be significantly different from a smaller consultancy, with significantly more support and more opportunity for variety. The downside is that you may have little influence over consultancy strategy, and little ability or opportunity to make any internal impact.

Structure	Description
Service Providers	Organisations in this category include global giants, such as Infosys, Capgemini, and Accenture, and the Big Four companies: KPMG, PWC, Deloitte, and Ernst & Young. In addition, there are thousands of smaller, local service providers in every region of the world. Here, consulting is one of many services provided. The advantage of a structure of this kind is the large variety or opportunity available (the ability to do things other than consulting). The downside may include a lack of real independence based on the commercial necessity to help other areas of the business.

Perspective 5 – Leverage

The fundamental strategy behind consultancy is the sale of your expertise, knowledge, or skills in the form of services. The price charged is set by calculating the value to the individuals of the time spent, plus an additional amount to cover the costs of running the business of the consultancy, and a further amount to ensure an acceptable amount of profit is achieved.

If you are a single, individual consultant, there are natural limits to how much time and effort you can spend on work, and therefore there are limits to how much the business can grow, and how much profit can be made. Some consultants are happy with this state of affairs, being content to spend time on activities they enjoy. They perform the roles they wish and turn down those they do not, not concerning themselves with growth beyond the personal. However, if you do wish to grow a business beyond these limits, then you have to work with others to magnify your skills. A small amount of personal effort in the form of direction, can be turned into a large amount of team effort when other individuals are used as levers to magnify the output. Within consultancy, this is the concept of leverage.

According to Jack Gabarro[1] (who built on the ideas of former Harvard Business School professor David Maister), consultancies fall on a spectrum that includes four types – rocket science, grey hair, procedure, and

[1] https://hbr.org/2021/03/what-professional-service-firms-must-do-to-thrive

commodity. The amount of leverage you require or can apply, depends on which of these four consultancy types you favour and aim to provide.

Consultant Leverage Spectrum

Type	Description
Rocket Science	A rocket science practice addresses idiosyncratic, bet-the-company problems that require deep expertise and creative problem-solving. This requires large amounts of your time and the least amount of leverage.
Grey Hair	A grey-hair practice provides seasoned counsel based on experience. It is possible to leverage this type of consultancy but only carefully and with lots of collaboration.
Procedure	A procedure practice offers a systematic approach to large, complicated problems that may not be cutting-edge but require attention to a plethora of considerations. More leverage can be applied to this type of consulting, focusing on the repeatable elements performed by more junior consultants.
Commodity	A commodity practice helps clients with relatively simple, routine problems by providing economical, expedient, and error-free service. Large amounts of repeatability mean the least senior oversight and the most leverage possibilities.

Perspective 6 – Ways of Working (Location)

At the time of writing, in June 2022, the world was still dealing with the devastating COVID-19 pandemic. The impact has been enormous, with billions affected and millions of lives lost. This has had huge consequences on the way people lead their lives and how they perform their work. The world of consulting had been affected like every other industry. As well as the challenges the pandemic introduced, there have also been changes that proved beneficial.

- In part due to the "Great Resignation" and reduced international mobility, clients are struggling to find employees of their own to perform certain roles, and they are turning to consultants, contractors, and professional services firms to fill this gap.

- Remote working has allowed clients to use expertise from around the world, potentially widening the market for successful consultants whilst simultaneously increasing competition in home markets.

- Clients are less insistent on the need for face-to-face contact, meaning sales, relationship building, and delivery activities are becoming more efficient.

- There are notable improvements in work-life balance across the industry as a result of remote working and a change in the acceptability of long working hours, mitigating some of the pressures that can come with consultancy.

The new normal is still being defined; therefore, consultants and clients are having to understand what works for both. This means agreeing upfront and putting the details into the contractual terms and conditions, making adjustments to pricing and fees to reflect increased costs, and being able to offer alternative services and delivery methods where they might decrease cost, add value, or increase choice.

Because of these changes, a new perspective has been established – **Ways of Working**.

- **Co-location.** Co-location with the client has been the default way of working for most consultants until COVID struck. It makes for easier collaboration and potentially easier access to information. And by being in view, it mitigates a common client fear of lack of control over the consultant's activities. However, this way of working has some downsides. It can be personally restrictive for you as the consultant, meaning a lack of control over where and when work is performed, and you may also face limitation on how you can manage other work outside of the individual client. For the client, it potentially restricts the amount of expertise on-site to those who are working locally or can be made to do so. There is potentially greater cost for either client or consultant due to the need to travel, and potentially a cost for the client in having to provide equipment on-site.

- **Remote.** At the other end of the spectrum from co-location is remote working. From a consultant's perspective, remote can mean work from home, from a consultancy office in another city, or even internationally. Through the ability to work remotely, the client has access to entirely new remote delivery models, which has the benefit of increased capacity and access to worldwide capability. Thereby, the consultant or consultancy can manage their own commitments in a more independent manner. It is important that all parties understand how reporting, relationships, and productivity are managed and ensured in remote working situations.

- **Hybrid.** Hybrid working is a way of working which mixes elements of co-location and remote. Theoretically then, hybrid working can be constructed to have the advantages of both models. For the individual, it allows the consultant an improved level of control, freedom, and individual work-life balance whilst allowing the benefits of face-to-face collaboration for both consultant and client. It is therefore a flexible model. There are some additional considerations, though. It requires the most upfront negotiation as to acceptable working patterns on both sides, and minds may change over time. You also need to coordinate with others on your project so your face-to-face time isn't someone else's remote time, and finally, you or the client may contend with the added costs of needing equipment in multiple locations.

Capability

What makes you unique as a consultant is your capability. No individual's capability is exactly the same as another's. Your capability is the combination of skills, abilities, and knowledge that you can bring to others through your role as a consultant. Continual change means it is a challenge to always have exactly the capability that is needed to deliver to all clients and to your market base. Capability, therefore, has to be assessed and developed continually to remain relevant to the varied roles and requirements demanded of you. Capability development enables you to execute your strategy, deliver your services, and keep up with the market. It is key to your reputation.

It is necessary therefore to have a robust process to do this. Without a process, your relevance is reduced, your ability to market or sell, compromised, and your services are weaker.

Capability development comprises four activities:

- Understanding your current capability. This requires defining, categorising, and rating the skills and knowledge relevant to your particular area of expertise.

- Setting capability targets. This comes through analysis of market drivers and trends, and then relating that back to you through setting objectives.

- Developing your capability – putting in place strategies, plans, and activities to meet the required capability.

- Demonstrating your credentials to show clients or potential clients that you have the knowledge, skills, and experience to make a difference to them.

Understanding your Current Capability

Because of the high demands on consultants to be adaptable and the innate variety of work, consultants need to develop capability across a wide number of areas. It is useful to think of this in two ways. First, the categories of skills, knowledge, and capabilities that adaptable consultants need to foster and gain, and second, the mechanism for quantifying these skills and tracking them over time.

To begin this model then, there are six categories of skills that consultants need:

- **Expert skills.** Most consultants are experts in a certain area, whether this be technical, business, or some other domain. A consultant needs to demonstrate their capability and they must keep up to date in their field. They use their specialised knowledge to craft solutions and add value. But it is not enough to simply have knowledge, this knowledge needs to be transferred. This means they require the ability to advise, instruct, and recommend in matters relating to their speciality.

- **Process skills.** Some consultants bring process skills rather than specific expertise. They can help the client achieve their own solution by using facilitation tools and techniques. Process consultants typically generate client-led solutions rather than consultant- or expert-led solutions. For this type of consulting, the consultant needs to show coaching, facilitation, and supporting skills. Process consulting can be the method used for a whole engagement, or it can be one technique used by expert consultants.

- **Communication skills.** Communication is the art of understanding and being understood. Writing, speaking, presenting, and listening skills are used day in and day out by all level of consultants. Good communication occurs when both parties agree that the message being sent is the same as the message being understood. It leaves both parties satisfied that there is common understanding.

- **Problem-solving skills.** Consultants need a range of thinking and understanding skills when performing expert or process consulting tasks because they regularly perform complex cognitive activities. Such skills include analytical and critical thinking skills to determine an accurate picture of any situation, as well as problem-solving and decision-making abilities to arrive at the correct solutions. Skilful consultants also make use of systems thinking to understand how complex organisations operate, and creativity techniques to help find exciting and relevant new approaches for clients.

- **Self-management skills.** Consultants need self-management skills. This is a wide category that focuses on the individual's ability to get the best out of themselves in the variety of challenging situations that consultancy brings. Good self-management means an individual performs well on a daily basis, across the length of a full engagement, and throughout their career. This leads to a number of positive states, including being motivated, confident, and resilient.

- **Collaboration skills.** Collaboration is the process of working effectively with others to bring the best out of them and yourself. Consultants move rapidly from team to team in their careers and often form part of multiple teams simultaneously. Consequently, good teamwork is essential. So, too, is the ability to influence. This is the ability to control the dynamics of a situation to the desired outcome. Which is important as consultants rarely have power – they need to use influence and exercise leverage to get things done. Positive relationships, empathising, and developing trust are key elements to building influence.

The following four skills: communication, problem-solving, self-management, and collaboration, are covered in detail in Chapter 5 – Abilities.

Tracking your Skills

Now that you understand the model, you need a mechanism or tool to enable you to assess yourself. Assessment allows you to baseline, identify weaknesses, and track positive progress as you work at improving your skills.

A skills matrix is a useful tool to help you rate yourself. Skills matrices are lists of skills broken down by category and scored using a simple scale such as 1 to 5. They enable you to baseline and then track the progress as you continually update the scores each time you develop deeper or new skills.

It is the expert skills that require most thought when performing this exercise. All other areas tend to be static in their definitions. For example, it will likely still be the same thinking skills needed in ten years' time. This is not the case for expert skills. These will change and build over time. For now, in this stage, it will suffice to list 10 to 20 skills in your field of expertise that you currently have, and then provide yourself an honest rating. You might also get someone else (perhaps a client whom you trust) to do this.

It is useful to think of the exercise in two ways. First, the categories of skills, knowledge, and capabilities that adaptable consultants need to foster, and second, the mechanism for quantifying and baselining these skills and tracking them over time. The skills matrix is a simple way in which you can do this for yourself, or for groups of others. Below is a very simple skills matrix that you can use to baseline your current consultancy skills.

Area	Skill
	Adaptability of communication style
	Writing
Communication	Document creation
	Speaking
	Presentation
	Analytical thinking
	Critical thinking
Problem Solving	Systems thinking
	Creative thinking
	Reframing
	Resilience
	Self-awareness
Self-Management	Learning
	Self-confidence
	Multitasking
	Teamwork
	Proactivity
	Adaptability of communication style
Collaboration	Humility
	Respect
	Recognition
	Cooperation
	Customer focus
	Value focus
Consultant Activities	Relationship building
	Knowledge management
	Professionalism

Setting Capability Targets

Once you have baselined your current technical and consulting capability, the next logical step is to assess how well your current capability matches the required capability. You can do this by going through a process of assessing where you need to be and comparing this to your current position. It is important to understand what expert capabilities you need to meet your strategic objectives, match client needs, and deliver your services.

Market research and market intelligence are useful concepts. Market research is the systematic gathering of data and information regarding the current state of the commercial market under view. Market intelligence takes this one step further, using market research to understand trends, make predictions, and look to the future.

Your market research and intelligence activities should include the following types:

- **Customer base.** Listening to your clients and contacts. This is one of the most effective ways of understanding what the market needs, and you should regard this as an absolutely essential activity. Even if your clients do not represent the whole market, they certainly represent the part of the market that is important to you.

- **Media.** Reading newspaper articles, trade press, newsletters, and social media will give you a wider view than that provided by just your customer base. Much media comes with its own agenda, and social media in particular tends to reinforce the opinions of those who read it. A wide base of media options will give you a more rounded view.

- **Research and advisory organisation.** If you have money to spend, you can engage specialist advisory groups, such as Gartner and Forrester, to provide advice. Their value proposition is market intelligence, and they spend considerable resources on not only collecting information but also analysing and predicting trends. Some material they provide is free, but access to their consultants and the best information is not.

- **Competitors.** Monitoring your competition may provide some indication of local or otherwise important trends. Websites, blogs, and social media provide significant sources of valuable insight into this group. Your competition, though, may react in different ways to you because of internal rather than external factors. Your strategy is not their strategy.

- **Surveys.** Occasional insight can be gathered from client and market surveys. Asking direct questions to a wide audience can mean a high amount of emphasis on specific issues that interest you. Surveys, however, typically have a low response rate, so don't expect too much from this route. In order to achieve sufficient success, keep surveys short, focused, and not so frequent as to become a burden.

- **Idea check.** Talking directly to your clients about your ideas, or going a step further with trial offers, will provide hard evidence from where it really counts – your clients. This type of "testing the water" allows you to put ideas to the test with minimum investment.

- **Focus groups.** Focus groups with members taken from current and potential client bases permit you to gather information in a setting which is more natural than interviews. By using open-ended questions to generate discussions, these "round table" events allow a wide set of viewpoints to emerge and have the added advantage of furthering relationships with and between participants.

Developing your Capability

After the process of capability baselining and target state analysis, you should put it to work. The point is to ensure *your* capability matches the *required* capability. To develop a capability effectively, a strategy is required. A capability development strategy comprises:

- **Capability principles/values.** These can be statements that clearly describe your underlying beliefs and behaviours that will drive all elements of the strategy.

- **Capability goals.** These should be both short and long term and should include measurable outcomes, such as specific qualifications and where the skills are used.

- **Capability development activities.** These include reading books and articles, classroom and online training, shadowing, and work experience. All activities should drive towards one or many of the identified goals.

- **Learning method.** A learning method is a set of repeatable steps that make learning more effective. The learning feedback loop is one such method and is a cycle of learn, do, listen, and think. Each activity feeds from and strengthens the previous one, and learning is complete when a learning goal is achieved.

- **Capability development plan.** A schedule or timetable can be as simple as a table with time across one axis and high-level subjects across the other. The schedule is filled out with topics, and this allows a high-level overview, a set of targets to aim for, and a way of measuring progress towards an overall goal.

- **Measurements.** You need a way of measuring how effective the learning has been. The skills matrix introduced earlier is the simplest way to do this.

The act of developing capability is never-ending. There is always a new technology, method, or tool that has been developed. Your strategy has to be assessed regularly. If you find that you have not made any adjustments to your goals or your plan in a year or more, then you are almost certainly missing something. Keep your plan up to date.

Demonstrating your Credentials

By following the process to this point, you will have baselined, analysed, and developed your capability, but for this to be of maximum effectiveness, it needs to be visible, and it needs to be demonstrated.

Demonstrating your capability is more than just telling people about what you are able to do. As a service provider, you don't really have something tangible to show. You have to show people your capability in subtle and not so subtle ways, so people can see and feel your experience and the value you could bring. It is necessary to show people your Credentials – your proof of capability.

Consider the following eight methods to help you present your credentials:

- **Qualifications and certifications.** Market or technical qualifications may be a threshold for acceptance of capability in some areas or professions. The weight they hold with clients varies considerably, but they are unlikely to harm your case for capability.

- **Value proposition.** Your value proposition is a way of expressing your capability which demonstrates clear benefits of your service to your customers. Creating and explaining your value proposition is a vital activity in capability demonstration and market differentiation.

- **Content and thought leadership.** Thought leadership is a way of adding value to your industry and your clients, through the creation and publication of educative or innovative material. Articles, books, blogs, and speaking at conferences are all ways of doing this.

- **Educating others.** Educating is one of the most effective and thorough ways of demonstrating your capability. Coaching, mentoring, training, or teaching are all distinct ways in which this can be done, and an effective consultant is conversant in all of these. *Education-based sales* is a sales strategy in itself and is predicated on the principle of continuous customer education. This encourages the customer to make their own informed decisions, all the while developing more and more trust in you, the consultant.

- **Marketing.** Marketing is about proactively selling and promoting your services and highlighting your capabilities. Marketing activities provide a valuable avenue for making yourself visible and generating business. Marketing is particularly valuable for trying to break into new domains or areas where relationships do not exist, and reputation has not yet been established. Marketing is discussed in more detail in the next section.

- **References.** Good reviews from previous clients, case studies, or other external mentions communicate capability without appearing self-congratulatory.

- **Data.** In larger organisations, or when you have completed many engagements, you may be able to quantify your achievements and publish this data.

- **Networking.** By taking advantage of opportunities to proactively meet with others in your industry, you raise your profile. In this way, potential clients and colleagues get to know about your experience and achievements as well as learn about you as an individual.

Services

Figure 4. Service Dimensions

Whatever type of consultant you are, whatever your specialism or the role you are taking on, and whatever your specific and unique combination of capabilities, there is one thing you will certainly be doing – and that is providing a service. A service is an expertise you can provide for a client because they have a need they cannot meet themselves. It is important to position yourself as someone who can meet a need by defining your services in a way that makes this clear.

This section describes a number of different but equally valid ways in which you may choose to define your services. There are three main dimensions you can use to classify the types of services you provide – client function (what business activity you perform), delivery method (how you do it), and consulting function (what consulting activity you perform). It is recommended that you consider using all of these ways in which to describe your services as they are relatively straightforward and complementary.

In addition, there are other ways that you may choose to define your services, depending on whether you have a specific capability or are aiming at a specific market segment. These include market aligned, intellectual property focus, domain, and technology.

Whichever one or combination of the above seven service dimensions you choose to use to define your services, the outcome you are after is the ability to demonstrate that you can solve the client's problem, match their requirement, or otherwise meet their need. It is important you be able to adapt and explain your services in a way that is relevant and pertinent to the client, given their unique set of circumstances. Sticking to one way and one way only will likely not get the outcome you are looking for.

Key Service Strategy 1 – Organise by Client Function

The first strategy is to define your services by referring to a business function. This is typically the simplest and most common method consultants use. For example, information technology services may be:

- Project management

- Business analysis

- Technical solutions

- Development

- Quality assurance

This provides a simple and clear description of the skills the consultancy holds and can bring to a client. Most importantly, this strategy uses language that clients understand. Services are described in a way designed to make it easier for the client and consultant to have immediate common ground because it typically matches industry process or model steps.

Service definition by function comes with quite a limitation as it embodies a very transactional view of consultancy with very little emphasis placed on the value proposition (that is, the overall value or benefit that a client enables by engaging with you). It also suits those clients who already know the answer to their problem (or think they do). By defining services in this way, you encourage this viewpoint. It is a simple and valid strategy, but many clients will be on the lookout for something more specific or relevant to them.

Over time, as consultants become more attuned to their client base and the needs of their target customers, it is common for this way of defining services to become less prominent as a strategy, perhaps combining with

THE CONSULTANT'S PLAYBOOK

other strategies. Marketing becomes more focused and small specialist units may form. With further time and increasing size, consultancies completely move away from this strategy and towards more customer-centric ways of organising and marketing.

Key Service Strategy 2 – Delivery Method

The second key service strategy is to focus on the delivery method. This strategy most accurately describes how the services are to be provided by focusing on the team composition, location, and interaction between client and provider. This type of categorisation is useful mostly in larger consultancy settings and less so where the consultant is solo or in a very small team. Services can be provided by means of several methods:

- **Resource augmentation** is the simplest. This involves providing an additional person or people to fill a specific gap in a team. Augmentation can be a single individual or a whole team and is characterised by minimal management from the consultancy and maximum management by the client. (This is sometimes referred to, oftentimes pejoratively, as "bodyshopping".)

- **Managed services** provide additional support to the client by continuing to oversee all the services, resources, or solutions put in place. This typically covers a spectrum of management ranging from regular meetings with the client to continual on-site management of delivered items. In addition, these services may also provide significant "value-add" through advice, consulting, or other support on top of the contracted work.

- **Partnership** is the term used to describe some client–consultancy relationships. This is usually an informal term where a client and consultancy work together for the mutual benefit of both parties. Partnerships are characterised by much closer working relationships, idea sharing, and an understanding that the commercial agreements are only part of the working relationship.

- **Outsourcing** is an extreme form of the managed services model where entire elements of a given business function are performed by an outside party. Outsourcing can be both a risk reduction and a cost-cutting activity. It enables clients to focus on their core competencies rather than trying to do everything.

- **Offshoring** is a version of outsourcing or managed services in which the service is delivered by 'out-of-country' elements. There can be cost advantages to a client through offshoring, though the distance and time difference add considerable risk if not managed correctly.

- **Nearshoring** is a variation of offshoring and has the same aims but is provided in the same country as the client or very nearby. It allows some of the cost benefits of offshoring but with less of the risks of work performed in other countries, and the communications or logistical challenges that it comes with.

- **Crowdsourcing** is a method of gathering resources by enlisting a large number of people, always remotely and possibly worldwide. This usually has a significant price advantage for clients, though it can be difficult to maintain quality oversight.

Categorising services by delivery method is often done if the client has a good understanding of what the services are but is looking for alternative ways to provide these services.

Key Service Strategy 3 – Consulting Function

The third and final key strategy is to focus on the consulting function, rather than the client function. As consultants are often engaged to perform certain activities, it may make sense to catalogue and describe these activities as services. It means clients have to understand your industry language, but once they do, you have another common vocabulary. Below is a non-exhaustive list of the activities that consultants perform:

- **Advisory** activities include pure consulting, that is, the processes of establishing the existence of a problem or other requirement and recommending a solution. This is in many ways the key core capability of any consultant.

- **Training** services allow a consultant to be able to transfer skills and knowledge to the client in an organised fashion.

- **Process improvement** is the analysis of current process with the aim of improving upon them. It is typically done as an activity against a standard, one that the consultant is familiar with, in the area they are expert in.

- **Audit** is a process of inspection to ensure that the areas under audit are accurate, complete, and documented. Consultants are good candidates to perform audits as they are typically both experts in the subject under audit and independent from the organisation.

- **Delivery** is the implementation of a solution. The consultant may have been involved in the creation of the solution, or this may have come about before the consultant's involvement.

One point of note with activity-focused services is that it does not give clients much view of what benefits they will get as a result of engaging. It is what you do, not what they get. As such, defining services in this way is becoming less common and is best if used in conjunction with other service focuses. Much of the early part of the consulting lifecycle is focused on matching your services with client needs so as to develop a suitable solution, but defining services only this way, may mean you do not even get to the point where you can have this discussion.

Other Service Strategies

Market Focus

This strategy defines services with regard to specialities or marketing activities. Describing services in this way is usually done to indicate that the consultancy's thinking is aligned with current marketing trends, the latest methodologies, or the client's own thinking. As such, it usually requires further clarification of exactly what this means to the client, or how it is to be delivered. Market-focused services might concentrate on:

- Current methodologies
- New technologies
- Other industry trends

Having your services focusing on current trends helps build an impression that you are an up-to-date, innovative consultancy, and it can give you plenty of fuel for marketing activities. This strategy, however, requires continual attention as the content becomes out of date or obsolete relatively quickly. It is best used in conjunction with one of the other key service focuses.

Intellectual Property

Intellectual property (IP) refers to creating new solutions and products which have value and need to be protected. By doing this you are potentially setting yourself up with a commercial advantage that will enable you to grow your business and profit directly from your knowledge.

IP or specialist services are those where the consultant has in-depth skills, sometimes unique and often in a niche area. These services do not have to be truly innovative or unique to qualify, but to be categorised as such, the services should be unique to you. The service should be rare or require highly skilled or informed resources (both people and knowledge).

Examples of an IP-based service can be products or processes you have developed, and which you control in terms of who may use or share them. Being unique or otherwise special, these services can be highly lucrative, especially if the service is leading the market. However, in order to remain so, the IP has to be kept current and ahead of other competitive offerings. Over time, others inevitably close some of the ground and the service becomes less valuable.

The fuel for IP-related services comes from the experience gathered during engagements. It is therefore of critical importance that you develop systems and processes to acquire, manage, and use knowledge.

Domain

Large consultancies often organise themselves around domain, sector, or industry. Although much consulting is the same across a sector, the culture, drivers, and economy usually vary tremendously by domain. In addition, clients themselves often insist on experience within their industry and as mentioned, with relevant technology, rather than consultants with generic consulting skills. The more demanding clients may even insist on experience with subsector and specific domain technologies (see the Technology section).

Standard industry sector lists exist to help you break down and define this. One is NACE (Nomenclature of Economic Activities), which is the industry standard classification system used in the European Union. This breaks down into the following 21 categories:

Category	Domain
A	Agriculture, Forestry and Fishing
B	Mining and Quarrying
C	Manufacturing
D	Electricity, Gas, Steam and Air Conditioning Supply
E	Water Supply; Sewerage, Waste Management and Remediation Activities
F	Construction
G	Wholesale and Retail Trade; Repair of Motor Vehicles and Motorcycles
H	Transportation and Storage
I	Accommodation and Food Service Activities
J	Information and Communication
K	Financial and Insurance Activities
L	Real Estate Activities
M	Professional, Scientific, and Technical Activities
N	Administrative and Support Service Activities
O	Public Administration and Defence; Compulsory Social Security
P	Education
Q	Human Health and Social Work Activities
R	Arts, Entertainment and Recreation
S	Other Service Activities
T	Activities of Households as Employers
U	Activities of Extraterritorial Organisations and Bodies

Defining your services in this way can be a good choice if you specialise or have substantial experience in a specific area. Depending on the area, this may provide you with a niche offering that others cannot match. Developing a specialist offering in an industry vertical can also be a very powerful move, especially if, as part of your business development strategy, you want to displace incumbent consultants or companies.

Technology

Just as clients demand specific domain experience when engaging consultants, they often demand experience with particular technologies, which increases the perceived likelihood of a successful change. Indeed, it is the consultant's experience with the particular technology that clients will seek if their own knowledge is lacking. This reduces their fear of uninformed consultants. Examples include:

* Customer relationship management (CRM)
* HR information systems (HRIS)
* E-learning
* Billing and payments systems

The advantage of defining services this way is that it becomes quite simple to explain what you do. If clients are asking for specific experience, a match will be clear to them. It should also be relatively straightforward for you to provide relevant examples of value delivered to clients in previous technology-focused engagements.

Clients

In consulting, the fundamental interaction is between two parties. The consultant being the first party and the client being the second. A client refers to the recipient of the knowledge and skills provided by a consultant. Simply put, the client is the customer of the consultant, and consultants would not exist without clients. There are four perspectives from which you can view this client–consultant interaction, and each gives you different considerations.

- The various roles clients play in their client organisation and the objectives they have in their interactions with you.
- The closeness of the relationship. Not all clients want very close relationships with their suppliers, so the key to this perspective is coming to a mutual understanding that works well enough for both parties.
- Their emotions, including motivations for, and fears of, working with you. There is an emotional context to taking advice from outside parties, which you need to be aware of and respect.
- The relationship quality and the importance that you can ascribe to the relationship.

Roles Clients Play

"Client" is a multi-use term, which refers to the recipient of a service provided by a consultancy, and which makes defining the client more complex than initially perceived. Sometimes your client is an individual; often, however, it is several people within an organisation. Complexity arises when these clients have different or opposing agendas.

In addition, the term "client" is applied to the wider organisation, in which case we can differentiate by referring to a client organisation. We can also refer to the client as the customer, although this description is not used to the same extent.

Two further definitions add to the complexity of defining the client. An individual client will have their own manager, who will at least be interested or possibly responsible for the relationship with the consultant. We need to consider this person as a senior client and attempt to build relationships with them, too.

Finally, we need to consider the financial client – this is the person who pays the bills. This person is typically one step removed from the initial client, but just as important, nonetheless.

These are the broad categories and definitions of a client. However, just as consultants perform differing roles, so too do clients, though compared to consultants, these are typically more firmly fixed and consistently performed. As a consultant, you need to identify who performs which role, bearing in mind that sometimes people perform multiple roles simultaneously. Neil Glass, in his book *Management Masterclass*,[2] identified six roles that individual clients play in the decision-making process:

- **The Authoriser** is not directly involved in decision-making but has the power to veto or sign off. It is important to identify and connect with these typically senior individuals to pre-empt contracting problems and wasted time.

- **The Owner** makes a decision or a recommendation. They are typically the party most affected by the decision. A relationship with the owner is the minimum needed to ensure success in enabling a commercial relationship.

- **The Gatekeeper** controls access to key parties, information, and resources. They can be an asset or a risk. An asset in that they will be able to provide introductions or information regarding who to contact, a risk if they feel their role is to prevent you from having this access.

- **A Key Influencer** will have a heavy sway over the owner and the resulting decision. There may or may not be a key influencer other than the owner, but if there is, you need to give them both the same focus and attention. A key influencer can be an obstacle but can also be a great ally.

- **An Influencer** is as above, but with less power to influence any decision.

- **The Technical Buyer** is a specialist who will be brought in to see if any technical solution the consultant recommends or provides is viable. Depending on what you are delivering, this may be a key contact later in the lifecycle. It requires a different mindset to relate to the technical buyer, who will wish to focus on the detail of the how, and less on the objective, benefit, or cost.

---

[2]   Glass, N. (1998). *Management Masterclass: A practical guide to the new realities of business.* Orion Publishing Company.

Closeness

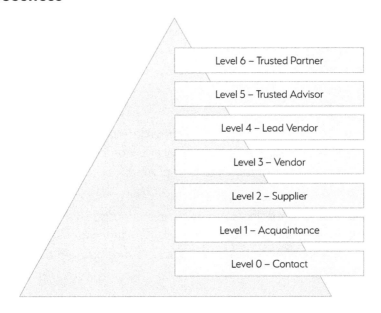

Figure 5. Client Closeness

The second key facet of client–consultant interaction is the level of closeness. We can define the closeness of the relationship with a simple model, where a higher score is given to a closer relationship. It is usual for consultants to want to move up the scale with their clients. Although, it is not necessarily the case that clients want to move up the scale with their consultants. In fact, larger clients typically want a range of closeness with consultants and vendors, with only the best, most proven at the highest levels. In some cases, especially amongst those clients with a strong internal bias, no supplier makes it to the higher levels.

The scale is as follows, from lowest to highest in level of closeness:

Level 0: Contact – Here the client is aware of the consultant but may not have ever met them.

Level 1: Acquaintance – The client has met with the consultant, possibly a number of times, though there is currently no commercial relationship.

Level 2: Supplier – The consultant performs occasional work, or has performed previous work, for the client. This level of engagement is characterised by single commercial contracts or service agreements, limited-service coverage for the consultant, and no internal sponsorship from client to consultant.

Level 3: Vendor – Now the consultant has a formalised relationship, characterised by Master Service Agreements, procurement involvement, and internal sponsorship into other areas. The consultant is one of a number of equally ranked suppliers.

Level 4: Lead Vendor – Here the consultant is the first choice for a client and sometimes, the only choice. To achieve this level takes time, trust, and a favourable track record.

Level 5: Trusted Advisor – To achieve this level of closeness, trust has been built over the long term, with the consultant able to tell careful truths and the client able to accept them.

Level 6: Trusted Partner – The pinnacle. The consultant is both external, through independent, expert status; and internal in nature, through having significant, almost irreplaceable client knowledge.

Emotions, Motivations, and Fears

The third key facet of the consultant–client interaction is formed by the emotional context. Sometimes there are clear reasons for clients to want to bring in outside parties. These are typically explicit needs to meet specific objectives or outcomes. There can, however, be a large number of underlying motivations for clients engaging with consultants. These include:

- **Emotional motivations,** such as the need to feel safe, or obtain sympathy, or to boost self-confidence or pride.

- **Personal motivations,** which include career development, to increase personal influence and power, to improve image, or for self-development reasons.

- **Rational motivations,** such as the need to innovate, to increase efficiency, or to improve reliability and performance.

- **Economic motivations,** including the desire to save costs or implement technical solutions, to improve processes, or to increase competitiveness.

As well as motivations, clients have fears when engaging with a consultant, such as the following:

Client Fears

Potential consultant incompetence	Consultants bring skills that aren't available internally. It is natural for clients to be uncertain until a consultant has proven their capability.
Loss of management control	Whilst a client wants a consultant to take responsibility (and sometimes accountability) for the assignment, they may subsequently feel excluded and deprived of control.
Continued dependency	Clients fear being unable to end a relationship, especially before having started. Consultants can mitigate this with upfront plans for knowledge transfer.
High fees	In comparison to internal costs, external rates can seem unreasonably high. Explanation is essential to ensure that the client understands the value delivered.
Inadequate consultant time to do the job	Clients face concerns that solutions delivery will take longer than expected due to poor expectation setting from early pre-sales activities.
Needing a consultant identifies management failure	By wanting to engage, a client has already identified a shortfall in capability. If consultants identify further shortfalls then, without the necessary care, the client's ego and position may be threatened.
Fear of disclosure of sensitive data	Clients want you to bring experience of similar projects, organisations, and their industry. However, they are rightly wary about having knowledge of their own organisation used elsewhere.
Improper diagnosis of client need	Clients don't want their unique and important problems to be reduced to an "off-the-cuff" diagnosis before proper analysis has been completed.

Partiality of the consultant	This is yet another paradox. Clients wish for alternative solutions and to understand what options they have, but too much pushing of products or services can be regarded with suspicion.

(Source: Tom Lambert, **High Income Consulting, 1999**)[3]

Recognising these underlying motivations and fears can be critical to successful engagements. Consequently, they should be brought to the surface, named, and acted upon. Surfaced motivations demonstrate that you have real understanding of the client's situation and have provided success criteria for the engagement, whereas surfaced fears are risks that need to be managed.

Relationship Levels, Quality, and Importance

An underlying premise for a successful consulting career is that the higher within a company you have established relationships, the more valuable they are. Access to more senior stakeholders means access to information about the client that is not always available lower down. Also, as strategy and direction are often delivered from the top down, you find yourself in a position of more influence with these higher levels of relationships.

Many consultants aim to have C-level or executive relationships, and whilst this is certainly beneficial, benefit can come from moving one level up from wherever your current relationships are. In fact, holding relationships at a number of levels is perhaps the most effective way to gain trust and influence outcomes.

Level

It is useful therefore to analyse and track the level of your relationships as well as the quality. As a broad generalisation, client relationships can be categorised as being at one of the following five levels: C-level/executive,

---

[3]   Lambert, T. (1999). *High Income Consulting: How to build and market your professional practice* (2nd ed.). Nicholas Brealey Publishing.

general management, middle management, programme, or team. In very simple terms, each level tends to have specific or typical drivers, and therefore your communication is most effective if it is directed towards these.

Level	Typical Drivers
C-Level/Executive	Strategy and governance
General Management	Cost and value
Middle Management	Organisation and capability
Programme	Delivery and speed
Team	Task and support

Quality

In addition, the quality of your relationships can be assessed. Each of the levels can be categorised as trusted, formal, or occasional. Of course, not every company is structured in a way that fits the model and not every relationship is so easily categorised, but relationship elevation is all about moving higher in the level of the organisation and moving to a higher quality of relationship.

Level	Description
Trusted	Regular weekly or two-weekly meetings with open channels for communication around this.
Formal	Meetings once a month, or based on otherwise agreed schedules and structured agendas.
Occasional	Irregular or ad hoc meetings which tend to be unstructured.

Importance

Finally, you may wish to categorise your individual client relationships by the degree of importance that it holds for you. Clients can come in a variety of sizes, from a single person to multi-billion-dollar international companies. And the larger the company, typically the larger the opportunity. However, understanding the importance of a client to you is a much more subjective exercise and is related to the consultant's own objectives as well as other factors. The importance of a client is potentially based on:

- The closeness of the relationships.
- The length of the relationships.
- The amount of trust that has been developed.
- How much the values of the two parties align.
- How well the objectives of the parties match.
- Past, present, and future value to both parties (including financial value).

These factors should all be considered when assessing relationship importance, and it should be regarded as a dynamic activity. You should look to reassess client relationship importance regularly.

Strategy

The final part of the Activate stage is focused on creating your strategy. The strategy is a set of choices which, when brought together, provide the direction for future actions, with the aim of increasing the likelihood of success. A strategy tells you where you are going and what you need to do to get there. It is a source of competitive advantage and a guide to refer back to for your planning.

Within *The Consultant's Playbook*, the strategy pulls together many of the topics and thinking covered in the previous sections of Activate, as well as other generic strategic thinking.

A process can be followed to ensure all elements relevant to consulting are covered. For the consultant, this is divided into two phases – Setting the Direction and Aligning the Plan. These two phases are done continually throughout the lifecycle of a consultancy at a regular interval, typically yearly.

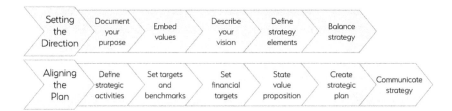

Figure 6. Strategy Process and Activities

Document your Purpose

The first part of creating a strategy can be described as **Setting the Direction**. Your purpose, values, and vision are considered and clarified before the individual strategic elements (consulting, capability, services, and clients – covered in the previous sections) are tackled.

The very first step in Setting the Direction is to document your purpose – that is, to define and elaborate on why you are providing consulting services. This purpose provides direction to all subsequent activities within the strategy and beyond.

Many organisations or individuals will use missions and visions to announce where they are going and why. The problem with these terms is that they lack a standard definition or criteria and are consequently used inconsistently or poorly. The concept of a company having a purpose has arisen as an alternative since it has a singular, clearer definition.

Your purpose is your most treasured and fundamental reason for doing what you are doing. It relates closely to your values (next section) and should be almost unchangeable over a long period of time. A person or company that does not have a clear purpose, risks lack of direction.

There are three levels of purpose to be considered when setting out as a consultant or forming a consultancy:

- **Individual** – What motivates you and why do you do what you do?
- **Corporate** – What is your company purpose and how do you help your customer?

- **Social** – How will your purpose help society and what specific social responsibility will you take?

There can be no conflict between the three if you are to succeed; they must be complementary and self-reinforcing.

Embed Values

Your values represent your fundamental beliefs. So intrinsic to your character that you would keep them even if they disadvantaged you compared to others. Values are key because they help alignment with other individuals, embed organisational culture, remind you and others of why you are consulting, and inspire you to the right decisions and behaviours.

The first stage in embedding values is to decide what the organisational values are. When creating your values, you should bear in mind the following:

- You should take input from multiple stakeholders in the organisation, so that the documented values truly reflect the organisational values. This helps to get buy-in from the organisation's stakeholders and increases the chance of successful implementation, adoption, and compliance.

In addition, if the values you are defining are for the entire organisation, there are some further considerations:

- You can use single words, but short sentences (not paragraphs) are better. Sentences provide more context and better realise the complexity and uniqueness of your organisational values. The values are therefore specific, not generic.

- Aim for between three to six values in total. Any fewer are unlikely to be broad enough to be effective and any more are not memorable.

- Values need to be applicable to all levels and roles within the organisation, not just the management layer, for example.

Once values have been decided on, take the following actions to make them a successful and fundamental part of the DNA of the business and ensure the values do not become diluted over time:

- Find opportunities to continually communicate the values.
- Monitor and measure progress and events against values.
- Refresh the values from time to time.
- Put initiatives in place to embed values into culture.
- Celebrate and reward good behaviour aligned to the values.
- Get regular commitment from the team to the values.

Describe your Vision (through Big Goals)

A vision statement describes the desired long-term results of your efforts. It is a single sentence (or possibly two), using clear, concise, and inspiring language that you, your clients, and everyone you work with can visualise. For a consultant organisation, this also has the advantage of allowing everyone to see how their efforts, whatever their role, contribute towards the greater vision. It is in line with your purpose and your values. It provides something for everyone to rally around.

When considering and documenting your vision as a consultant or for a consultancy, you should consider the following:

- Consultancies are people businesses that deal with other businesses, so it would seem wise to consider these elements in a vision statement.
- You may consider describing the impact you want to make on the world, how you interact with clients and the industry, and what type of culture you want to foster.
- You should use it to differentiate from competitors.
- The horizon for the vision should be at least five to ten years in the future. Some writers suggest the vision should have an even longer horizon; however, within the consultancy industry sector even five years can see significant change, which might require you to adapt your vision to accordingly anyway. Nonetheless, you should use the opportunity to state ambitious goals, focusing on a successful future.

Once the vision is agreed, you should detail the vision with goals. This is important because it is difficult to get a 20-word vision statement to cover all the intricacies and stages of what you want to do, and what needs to happen. Therefore, goals are important because they provide the extra internal detail you need to make the vision a reality. When creating goals for your vision they should be:

- **Long-term goals** to match your vision horizon and not short-term targets which will be covered in financial or strategic initiatives planning.

- **Challenging** to keep you and the team moving forward and focused on bigger things. The goals should stretch your capability, but not be completely unachievable.

- **Simple** to understand, specific, and measurable, again using clear language so that they are motivating for you and others.

Define Strategy Elements

You now have your purpose, your values, and your goals. Next, you need to consider how you are going to achieve your goals. This means first considering each of the individual strategy elements below, which will build to set the overall direction, before considering the detailed activities that will help you achieve your strategy.

This exercise can be broken down by considering several strategy groups that are aligned with the earlier sections. When considering each of the questions, you should do this in parallel with the relevant parts in the book.

Document Consulting Strategy

Your consulting strategy should answer the following questions:

- What is your core capability?
- What are the roles that you are capable of and willing to play?
- How will you position yourself?
- What is the corporate structure of your organisation?
- How much leverage will you use?

Document Service Strategy

Your service strategy should answer the following questions:

- What do you deliver for your client?
- How do you deliver it?
- Are there specific activities you perform that you wish to highlight?
- Are there specific niches you cater for, such as domain or technology?

Document Capability Strategy

Your capability strategy should specifically answer the following questions:

- What capabilities will be needed right now and in the immediate future to deliver your goals?
- How will you continually ensure you understand what capability is required to meet future demands and requirements?
- What measurements will you put in place?
- How will you develop your capability to match this?
- How will you augment your capability if you are not able to provide it all yourself?

In addition, if you are looking at leveraging others as part of your business strategy, you will need to consider the following:

- How will you plan for workforce demand and supply in the short, medium, and long term?
- How will you source and deliver capability?
- What is your people management approach and organisational structure?
- How will you articulate your employee value proposition (EVP)?
- Are there any specific retention activities to be put in place?
- How will you enable and measure organisational efficiency?
- How will you ensure that non-billable resources are managed effectively and efficiently to the benefit of the overall business?
- What resource provisioning and allocation strategies and processes will be in place?

Document Client Strategy

Your client strategy should answer the following questions:

- Which clients or domains will you target?
- What level of client will you engage with?
- What is your message to your clients?
- How do you organise yourself?
- What is your strategy for growth?
- How would you segment your market?
- How close to your client do you hope to get?

Document Generic Business Strategy Elements

The previous sections, relating to Consultant, Capability, Services, and Clients have been specifically called out as requiring attention because they are fundamental to consultants and consultancy. In addition, there are other general business function strategies that you may wish to consider at this stage.

The following list is not complete but provides a good starting point:

- Financial, such as revenue and profits targets, invoicing, and investment.
- Growth, including sales method and process, and marketing strategies.
- Operations such as human resources, including policies and health and safety, information technology, and communication.

Balance Strategy

Once all the individual strategy groups have been considered and individual strategy elements have been documented, a certain amount of balancing is necessary to ensure the elements are all complementary and appropriately prioritised. There may be too many or too few for you to manage or focus on. They may be too skewed towards one area or perhaps too widely spread. The value from certain activities may not be sufficient for the investment that would be needed, or there may be dependencies between activities or dependences on outside influences which need to be considered.

In addition, it is at this point that questions of balance regarding the operations and focus of the business should be considered. Such questions have to be addressed to minimise the risk of being pushed by circumstances into dangerous situations or defaulting to certain behaviours. It is not unusual that as consultancies grow, they become unbalanced. They are pushed into a certain direction by outside forces. And while this lack of balance can be managed, the consultancies are prevented from attaining the success that they could otherwise achieve and eventually, without intervention, things can fall over. It is better to begin by considering the questions that will continually come up during the lifetime of a consultancy. The elements to balance include the following:

- Working *in* the business (delivering to clients) or *on* the business (delivering to your own business).
- Profit with purpose.
- Growth (finding new clients) or on-service (working with existing ones).
- Hiring to increase capability or training existing employees.
- Organic growth or acquisition.
- Self-funded or externally financially supported.

Define Strategic Activities

So far, within this section, we have considered setting the direction, that is, understanding, deciding, and setting the trajectory for the business of being a consultant. Once this is done, the plan is developed during a more detailed exercise and is aligned with the direction. This step includes defining the activities and tasks, benchmarking – including setting targets and measurements, setting financial goals, putting your value proposition into words that resonate with potential clients, creating your strategic plan, and finally, communicating your strategy. In larger organisations, the steps performed so far are usually driven from the top down. Executive team members set the direction. **Aligning the Plan**, however, is a more collaborative exercise involving wider stakeholder groups and those who are involved in implementing the plan.

The first activity in aligning the plan is to define the strategic activities that will help you meet the strategic objectives. As an initial activity, consider and document any influences on the strategy, from both an internal and external perspective. These include:

- Internal dynamics and considerations, such as organisational structures.
- Market movements.
- Client strategies.
- Competitor activities and strategies.
- Constraints, such as your financial position.

Strategic initiatives are projects in which money is invested to improve the key functions of the organisation and thereby provide a positive return on investment. A small number of focused and carefully chosen initiatives can advance your long-term interests. Care should be taken not to choose too many initiatives (thus taking focus away from revenue-generating activities) or risky initiatives (which may not deliver any benefit or may not be completed if you do not have the capability).

The table below includes several useful strategic activity categories that should be considered for action. When documenting each activity, include the responsible party, target dates, and measurement/success criteria.

Activity Type	Description
Solutions	An overarching term for activities that meet a perceived need.
Accelerators	A particular solution that speeds up a given activity.
Innovation	A solution that is novel within the market and will be pitched as such.
Product	A self-contained and easily implementable solution (sometimes *solution* is also used in this context).
Efficiency Opportunities	Internal solutions to reduce the effort or cost of existing activities.
Market Openings	A newly recognised need in the market that should be analysed for rapid exploitation.
Enablers	An activity or solution whose value is in unlocking value elsewhere.
Tools	Primarily software that supports the business and enables a variety of improvements.
Process Improvements	Changes to ways of working that result in benefits such as increased speed or reduced work – these can be business or client focused.
Organisational Improvement	Changes to structure, roles, or functions for management or delivery.
Capability Uplift	Improving skills or additional services to help meet market need.
Geographical Expansion	Setting up a unit or a business presence in a new region.

Set Targets and Benchmarks

As part of planning, mechanisms should be put in place to understand the health and performance of the overall business. Measurements, often known as key performance indicators (KPIs), allow you to monitor and react to specific and clear data to adjust tactics or execution to achieve your strategy and maintain your direction.

A balanced scorecard is one useful way in which to do this. This method promotes alignment with strategy, and it widens the definition of business performance/success to encompass more than pure financial mea-sures. In larger consultancy teams, it promotes top-down consistency of behaviour and can be used to incentivise individual performance. The aim of the scorecard is not to measure everything but to measure those things which have the greatest impact on business performance.

To create a balanced scorecard, we look at four interrelated dimensions of business performance and create indicators and measurements for these:

- **Financial** – To succeed financially, how should we appear to our stakeholders?

- **Customer** – To achieve our vision, how should we appear to our customers?

- **Operational** – To satisfy shareholders and customers, what internal elements must we excel at?

- **Learning and growth** – To achieve our vision, how will we sustain our ability to change and improve?

An example balanced scorecard with 13 elements across the four dimen-sions appears below:

Element	Vision	Measurement
Gross Revenue	Revenue grows above market growth	20% revenue growth in the next 3 financial years
Gross Margin	Excellent margins are achieved and maintained using the right services	35% margin
Customer Satisfaction	We are seen as leaders in the field, always providing quality services	Customer satisfaction of 90%
Customer Value	Clients focus on the value that has been added, not the cost	Discounts from rates provided < 10% of time
Service Alignment	We understand our clients' needs and supply the right range of services	We have a service coverage score of 75%

Element	Vision	Measurement
Utilisation	There is efficient utilisation of our employees	Between 86% and 90% operational utilisation
Turnover	We have the "right" amount of attrition in the wider organisation	< 15% annual turnover
Mobility	We have a highly mobile workforce in the wider organisation	25% of workforce are mobile for period of 3 months or longer
Employee Engagement	Work is engaging and satisfying	Employee engagement score > 8/10
Client Relationship	There are systems, which are effectively used, that allow us to manage client relations	99% of opportunities are recorded in the CRM within 48 hours
Service Capability	Our consultants have a high level of knowledge and understanding of the services portfolio	All consultants have completed the Consultancy Service certification
People Capability	Appropriate skills and continual learning. We have systems to measure skills that are used	65% of consultants trained in the financial domain. 100% of consultants have updated skills data
Knowledge Management	There is a high amount of sharing and reuse of knowledge	90% of consultants have accessed and deposited information into the knowledge management system

Set Financial Targets

The balanced scorecard is important because it provides an alternative to simply measuring success in financial terms. Without financial success, however, your business may not be sustainable. Your targets for financial growth are therefore a key consideration. At this stage in the planning phase, you should first focus on the planned for revenue or income figures, and not the profit figures. Profit will be a function of several factors, including commercial agreements, rates, and efficiency. Targets for this "bottom line" are set during separate budgeting exercises.

There are several methods to create your top revenue targets:

- **Top-Down.** Increment based, where targets are set by adding an increment, such as a percentage, to what was achieved in a previous period. Typically, the larger the company, the smaller the percentage increment will be.

- **Bottom-up.** Pipeline based, where targets are set using a detailed approach of demand planning, based on known pipelines in existing clients, as well as business development targets.

- **Stretch and aspirational.** Where targets are set top-down to encourage ambitious or even aggressive growth, not necessarily in an effort to attain the targets, but rather to attain greater performance than a moderate or business-as-usual approach might.

You should also consider your horizon. Fundamentally, the shorter the horizon, the firmer your numbers should be. Conversely, the longer the horizon, the less certain the numbers are likely to be, and the more likely they are to be adjusted as the horizon comes into view.

A dual-horizon approach to financial projection can be used, where "hard targets" are set for performance to be measured against, and "soft targets" are set to be used for planning purposes. As the horizon approaches, the soft targets are adjusted and become hard targets, and further soft targets are created. A standard approach, therefore, might set hard targets for three-, six-, or twelve-month horizons, and soft targets for anything up to three to five years.

At this time, you are only considering the top-line numbers. To create a valid budget, a detailed and separate budgeting process will need to be completed. This has several purposes, including specifying the additional detail that is needed to run the business and manage cashflow. It also provides a sanity check on the strategy. Adjustment to target, especially if these numbers are aspirational, is to be expected.

State the Value Proposition

A value proposition is a statement or short description that encapsulates the value that you will provide to those who engage with you. It is a key way of understanding, demonstrating, and communicating what makes you attractive to clients. It is used to convince clients why they should use your services or solutions. Formulating your value proposition at the strategy stage is a useful activity because it forces you to understand whether your strategy is sufficiently client-focused and easy to communicate. Both attributes are vital because for many consumers, your value proposition is the very first contact point with you and your brand, and it has an outsized effect on your success.

An effective value proposition has several qualities:

- **Client-value focused.** It is connected to your target client's problems. It addresses the client's wants (emotional drivers), needs (rational motivators), and fears (undesired outcomes).
- **Specific not general.** It clearly refers to you and cannot be confused with other service providers.
- **Differentiates from competitors.** It describes a clear difference between you and your competition.
- **Substantive.** It can be backed up by proof or consultant case studies or external analysis.
- **Proven.** It has been tested, both internally and externally, so that it demonstrably resonates.

Below are three possible formats for creating your value proposition:

- **List of benefits.** One option is to have a headline followed by paragraph. The paragraph can be a list of benefits that clients accrue when engaging with you.
- **Single line.** A second option is a simple sentence with the following format: "I help X do Y by doing Z". This is a good format for an individual (thanks to Steve Blank).[4] For example, my goal for this book is

---

[4]   https://steveblank.com/2011/09/22/
how-to-build-a-web-startup-lean-launchpad-edition/

to allow professional consultants to make a difference for themselves, for their clients, and for their business by providing the tools they need.

- **Triple theme.** A third option (known as the Harvard Business School Method)[5] leads to a multi-stranded value proposition, arrived at by brainstorming around the following questions: Which customers are you going to serve? Which needs are you going to meet? What relative price will provide acceptable value for customers and acceptable profitability for the customer? Together, the three create a triangle which provides the material for a rounded and succinct value proposition.

Create your Strategic Plan

During the planning phase, you need to be able to explain and communicate the detailed ways in which you are striving to deliver your strategy. The strategic plan is one such way. This is a document that includes the key topics that all consultants need to consider. Plus, it encompasses all the planning and thought done so far during the two phases of Setting the Direction and Aligning the Plan, presented within this chapter.

The format and contents for a strategic plan are described in the table below:

Section	Description
Consultancy Background	A high-level description of how the consultancy came to be. Background can give insight to outside parties and lays foundations internally.
Purpose	The fundamental reason why you are in business.
Values	Your fundamental beliefs as an individual and for the organisation, which drive behaviour and culture.
Vision	The desired long-term results of your and your company's efforts.
Goals	Measurable outcomes that detail the vision.

---

[5] https://www.isc.hbs.edu/strategy/creating-a-successful-strategy/Pages/unique-value-proposition.aspx

Section	Description
Consultancy Strategy	How you perceive your role as a consultant, and how you will present yourself to the market.
Capability Strategy	How you will develop and monitor your capability, and the capability areas you will focus on.
Services Description	A description of how you define and categorise your services.
Client Strategy	How you will target and interact with potential and current clients.
Value Proposition and Benefits	A condensed and easy-to-understand statement to explain why clients should choose to work with you and what the benefits are.
Management and Organisation	A high-level description of how the management of the organisation is structured, and the given responsibilities of the key roles.
Strategic Activities	A list of strategic activities to improve the business, including description, responsible party, success criteria, and timescales.
Financial Targets	Revenue targets for a specified timeline (usually from one to three years).
Activity Roadmap	The visual representation of elements of the business plan against a timeline. It includes financial targets, strategic activities, and other goals. It can be used as an executive or employee summary tool.

It is advised that the plan goes through a review and feedback process. It is not necessary to sign off the plan; instead, you are advised to consider it a working document that should be amended when the situation demands it.

Communicate your Strategy

Your colleagues, your clients, and even your industry all have interest in your approach and strategy. Without understanding your values, purpose and vision, these other stakeholders will not truly understand what you can offer them now and in the future.

This situation gives rise to the challenges of buy-in and commitment. A concerted effort to communicate your strategy and your strategic plan is a fundamental part of the strategy itself. Communication of the strategy should be continually addressed, so it is worth including formal communication on the strategy at the following stages, in addition to continual informal communication:

- During the strategy creation process. By setting out the strategy creation process transparently and allowing your colleagues or clients input into it, you are creating the environment for increased buy-in and a more effective deployment of the strategy.

- As part of the finalisation and agreement of the strategy. Review and feedback both increase buy-in and provide an element of testing of the strategy. A wide audience of colleagues, clients, and other market stakeholders will provide a level of certainty that the strategy is valid.

- At regular intervals in order to communicate progress against the strategic plan. The strategy needs to live and breathe to be real to stakeholders. Reference against the goals on a regular basis and share the performance outcome with a wide audience; it will allow you to maintain the strategy as a central focus for everyone's actions.

Ways in which to communicate the strategy or its elements include:

- Publication of the strategy document.
- Publication of the roadmap element of the strategy.
- Roadshows and workshops to enable face-to-face presentation to stakeholders.

Key Practice 1 - Marketing

Marketing is proactively promoting yourself, your services, and your capabilities. With the right marketing activities, delivered in the right way, and to the right quality, you will generate increased visibility and improved engagement with potential leads. The accompanying benefit will be an increase in the number of consulting opportunities.

Marketing is particularly valuable when trying to break into new domains or areas where relationships do not exist, and reputation has not yet been established.

There are several benefits to marketing yourself and your services:

- **To efficiently highlight who you are, your services, and your capability.** Having valuable and interesting content in front of potential clients helps demonstrate your capability and makes you easier to find.

- **To increase your visibility.** Most people have multiple things vying for their attention and you are not top of mind! Marketing, if done well, is one channel to increase awareness.

- **To increase your perceived value.** High-quality marketing, where relevant high-quality content is provided, increases the perception of the value you are adding, even more so if it comes with no strings attached.

- **To engage with current and potential clients.** A response from a marketing activity can quickly turn into a conversation, possibly leading to a commercial or professional relationship.

Ultimately, the point of almost all marketing is to increase the chances of opportunities for sales so you can generate income and further success in your career. But your potential marketing targets are likely to be a wide spectrum of personality types. Consequently, you require a range of marketing activity options to engage as many personality types as possible, thereby maximising your effectiveness.

Ten Ways to Market Yourself

As a consultant, it is delivery work that is likely to take the largest proportion of your time. Marketing is one of those activities that has to be accommodated in the time remaining. The activity or activities you implement should focus on providing a large amount of benefit in a reasonable amount of time. There are several different ways of doing this:

- **Website.** As well as providing a shop window for your services, websites can generate passive income. Videos, documents, templates, or other IP elements can be offered for free or for a price.

- **Content.** Books, articles, blogs, and newsletters all fulfil the same purpose of keeping your name in front of your clients and your prospects. Well-written and informative books can lend you an air of gravitas, but some of the same benefit can be gained by publishing articles or regularly producing your own blog, podcast, or webinar, and distributing newsletters or social media output regularly.

- **Conferences.** Conferences provide three avenues for marketing. You can land a speaking slot. If you can tolerate speaking in front of potentially hundreds of people, this will provide a high-profile opportunity for you and your brand. You can attend and use the opportunity to network and promote yourself and your services. You can have a stall, which is usually a paid marketing opportunity, to present material and talk about your services to a potentially interested audience.

- **Training courses.** You can deliver paid or free courses or sessions. These can be face to face or remote. Educating others is one of the most effective ways of demonstrating your capability.

- **Networking.** Attending professional or relevant semi-social meetings is an exercise in increasing your profile. It pays greater dividends to attend events that are not simply meetings of your own work community, but rather other business communities, which may provide opportunities to expand your network.

- **Campaigns.** A marketing campaign is a coordinated set of marketing activities that typically revolve around a chosen theme and a variety of different events. These have specific objectives and finite timescales. There are three types of marketing campaigns worth considering for consultants: a mass marketing campaign where a generic offer is made to a wide audience, usually via e-mail; a tailored marketing campaign where there is tailoring of the message to individually chosen recipients; and a tailored sales campaign where individuals are directly targeted for general introductions to you and your services.

- **Brochures.** Brochures and statements of capability perform similar functions but tend to differ in their production quality. A brochure is typically at the higher and more expensive end, whereas a statement of capability is easier to produce and less costly. Both list and describe the services you provide and may include biography or case study details.

- **Social media.** This is a critical marketing activity in a digital marketing world. Social media marketing allows an element of interactivity that other marketing methods may not. It also allows you to drive traffic to your website and, because analytical tools are available, perform analysis on those interactions. Strong and engaging content is key to successful marketing for consultants as much as for anyone else.

- **Mail.** In an era of digital communications, mail is paradoxically made more effective by its rarity. Assuming the message contained is of use, hard copy material can be impactful, even more so if it is matched with a personal, even handwritten message.

- **Case studies.** In the world of professional services, a case study (or testimonial) is a description of previous engagement, designed to showcase achievement. They may include a problem statement, how the problem was solved, and the benefits or value achieved by the client. Named case studies (where the client has agreed to put their name to it) might also include quotable statements.

The choice of which marketing activities to perform is dependent on whichever you believe will be effective in meeting the objectives you have set. Large potential audiences are likely to be differently receptive to each possible activity. A certain amount of trial and error is necessary, and any marketing process should include a retrospective to see what worked and what did not.

Principles of High-Quality Marketing for Consultants

Over time you will likely find the right combination of high-quality marketing activities for your audience, but whatever the marketing method, there are some principles that will help it to be effective and successful.

Conversely, as well as being a waste of time and having significant opportunity cost and real cost, poor marketing can be damaging – poor quality marketing indicates poor quality delivery.

Marketing should be:

1 **Targeted.** Marketing should be relevant by being aligned to the client need. It should also be aligned to the market need as derived from your market research and market intelligence gathering.

2 **Tailored.** Your communications should feel personal and considered, as well as relevant to the recipient.

3 **Efficient.** By using templates to get high-quality, well-constructed marketing, which include consistent key messages, you will speed up the time required to construct broad-based marketing campaigns.

4 **Directed.** By keeping the message directed towards your avatar (your ideal customer), you make sure the message is efficiently focused.

5 **Clear.** The message should be easy to understand, both in visual composition and verbal construction. It should be concise and well framed because you are vying for attention with messages from many other sources.

6 **Reflective of you.** As an individual or sole consultant, your marketing should focus on your strengths and be in keeping with your values and desires. Write your content to fit your style, and ensure it is a match with your capability. Should you then be asked to deliver something off the back of a successful campaign, you will be able to meet the client's expectations.

7 **Regular.** To be effective over time, your marketing should be continual (but not overwhelming). Weekly or bi-weekly emails are probably optimum – if this can be sustained – since it gives the impression of high productivity and vibrancy.

8 **Engaging.** Marketing should be attractive, with a good hook. This means it may be innovative but practical, unusual enough to be remarked on, or educational in nature.

9 **Focused on value and benefit.** You should communicate a clear set of benefits from performing the action suggested, taking up the offer

or otherwise, following the message. Describe both tangible (monetary) and intangible benefits. You may wish to highlight what makes you different from your competitors in this context.

10 Embedded with a call to action. Make sure the audience knows what to do in order to reap the benefits of the information. This might be a set of steps that they are able to perform on their own, or that they may need your help with.

2
ACQUIRE

Sales	Contracting

Figure 7. The Consultant's Playbook Structure – Acquire Steps and Activities

The Activate chapter has laid the groundwork for the next step, Acquire. It is at this point that you articulate your services, and the benefits they can deliver, to eventually reach an agreement with a client to work together. The Acquire process includes two core elements – Sales and Contracting.

Sales

The objective of this step is to generate leads and create opportunities for you to deliver consulting engagements. You do this by contacting potential clients so they might consider your services and doing business with you.

Sales as an activity, typically precedes any of the other activities in the formal consulting process, though it can continue to occur in parallel as further opportunities are explored. In larger organisations, this activity may be performed by a separate sales or account function. In smaller organisations, it is often performed by the same individual who delivers the services.

Many consultants will feel uncomfortable with the prospect of having to sell. But sales and consulting are almost inseparable. This discomfort may be reduced if you consider sales as a process to be followed – and consultants love process!

There are three activities performed sequentially within the Sales step:

1 **Generating and managing leads.** A lead is an individual or an organisation that might be interested in your services, but at this point you do not know exactly what the situation may be or what that interest is. The three categories of leads that consultants encounter can be classified as "reactive" (inward), "proactive" (outward), and "competitive" (inward or outward where multiple suppliers are following up).

2 **Establishing the opportunity.** Once a lead is generated, that lead needs to be followed up to explore if there is a real need for any of the services you provide.

3 **Qualifying the opportunity.** Qualification is the process of understanding whether the consultant or consultancy are capable of, and willing to, provide a solution, and whether the consultant believes that the other party is sufficiently committed to the process.

Step 1 – Generating and Managing Leads

A lead is an individual or an organisation that might be interested in your services, but at this point you do not know exactly what their situation may be or what level of interest there is. Leads come from several directions, and there are three categories of leads to consider: reactive leads – where you react to someone else contacting you, proactive leads – where you actively generate a lead, and competitive leads – which are generated for multiple suppliers to pursue.

Examples of reactive leads include:

- **Enquiry.** Website enquiries or phone calls generate leads from parties who know little about you.

- **Introduction via a contact.** A colleague or other client may provide a mutual introduction. Since these leads are as a result of someone vouching for you and your services, they can be very effective.

- **Introduction or referral via an existing client.** This is particularly effective as the client knows your capability first-hand and provides a de facto reference in doing the hand-off.

- **Call from a previous colleague or relationship.** This type of lead means much of the required groundwork is done, and therefore the trust and relationship is very much in place.

- **Introduction via a partnership.** Strategic partnerships can be developed for the mutual benefit of both organisations. Leads through this channel may come with the other partnership party's expectations of mutual benefit.

Examples of proactive leads include:

- **A cold call.** These are unsolicited calls or visits to parties who have not previously expressed any interest in your services. To be effective, you would need to believe that they may have a potential interest in or need for your services – if they were to know more about you and your capabilities.

- **A call to a previous relationship.** This type of lead is the warmer equivalent of the cold call. The maintenance and use of these business relationships is a mainstay of the consulting business and should be pursued regularly.

- **A contact at a conference stand.** Having a stand at a relevant conference will generate leads, though the cost of the exercise, often measured in thousands of dollars, is not guaranteed to be covered by the business generated.

- **A contact from a campaign.** This could be as a result of the specific offer or general increased awareness of you and your services, generated from any of the three described marketing campaign types.

- **A contact as a result of a speaker slot.** Speaking at a conference is a good showcase for your capability and knowledge, though a weak presentation may cause more damage than benefit!

Examples of competitive leads include:

- **Government and supplier panels.** Many organisations will manage their requirements though panels of suppliers. Getting on to these panels can be a prerequisite for working in such areas. Leads from this source are often very strong and may be classed directly as opportunities.

- **Marketplaces.** A marketplace is like a shop window. It is a panel of consultants or consultancies who present their services in a cen-tralised portal, and buyers can purchase knowing that the terms and conditions (and typically prices) have been set in advance. It also means that any due diligence has been performed and therefore the buyer can have a reasonable confidence that the provider can pro-vide what they say, speeding up the process for both.

- **Requests for proposals (RFPs).** The bane of many consultants' exis-tence. These require a large amount of effort for both parties and are often very competitive. Considerable thought needs to be put into qualification (see later), particularly whether the effort is worthwhile, before any lead is pursued.

To maximise your chances of developing business, it is important that you keep all lead generation activities centrally recorded and thereby build your pipeline. The larger your pipeline, the larger the number of opportunities and the more opportunities, the more sales. This can be done using a customer relationship management (CRM) system or failing that, using a simple spreadsheet or database.

Step 2 – Establishing the Opportunity

Once a lead is generated, follow up on it to explore if there is a real need for any of the services you provide. If, once the exploration has been completed, there is a need, a fit with your services, and sufficient interest, then your lead has now led to an opportunity. An opportunity is therefore a lead with a reasonable potential of becoming a client.

Arranging to Meet

To convert any lead into an opportunity, the first step is often to meet. You may have already met, perhaps when introduced or when the initial contact was made; however, you need to formally assess whether there is a real need to be investigated and a mutual desire to progress down this path. It is worth noting that not all leads will follow this pattern exactly. RFPs, for example, follow a strict client-defined path and process to ensure a level playing field. Panels and marketplaces also have defined engagement procedures.

For the leads without such structure, the meeting is a critical step in the process as it is here where the first real steps in relationship building occur. Therefore, face-to-face contact is important because it is hard to build a relationship and develop sufficient trust without at least some level of personal contact. In fact, it is quite unlikely that the opportunity will go anywhere without this, though video has proven to be arguably as effective a way of meeting as physically doing so, especially if distance is a factor.

If you are unable to arrange a meeting, then this may mean either that there was never really much of an opportunity in the first place, or alternatively, that something has gone wrong. It is worth asking the question of your lead to make sure that you are not missing something obvious, or if there may be another way of approaching the problem that might be successful.

There are a number of logistical considerations in making the appointment to meet:

- **Timing.** Unless the contact has arranged a specific time, it is up to you to do this. It is perhaps best to offer a range of available times to make it easier for the other party. You may need to arrange things weeks or even months in advance. In the long run, it pays to be flexible, which may well result in added respect and trust between you and your client.

- **Duration.** You are usually faced with two real options: 30 minutes or one hour. Less than this may indicate the low priority you or your lead place on the potential opportunity, and any longer than an hour may be onerous. But there is a third option: the 45-minute meeting. This has the advantage of seeming less onerous than the full hour meeting, but in actuality, it can carry on for this length of time since few people plan to do anything with the remaining 15 minutes.

- **Venue.** Your office, theirs, or a neutral venue? Offices provide more formality and privacy, while neutral venues, such as coffee shops, provide less privacy but more of a relaxed vibe. Cultural norms vary from country to country, and industry to industry, and need to be understood to make the right choice. If in doubt, let the other party choose.

- **The content and style of your invitation.** A calendar invitation is better than an email, and the tone should be friendly but professional. In addition, any communication should be easy to read and free of errors. It is useful to have a template that can be personalised. Finally, adding some judicious descriptions (without bragging) of relevant previous engagements, allows the client to see your credentials and realise that it might be a wise choice to select you. By following this format, it means you do not have to spend the first five or ten minutes of any meeting trying to sell yourself, rather than listening to the client.

Groundwork

Prior to the meeting, you may wish to do some research into the person or people you are meeting. You do want to exercise a light touch, of course, so as not to be intrusive, insensitive, or otherwise inappropriate. The research can be done via social media analysis, or by Googling them, or by talking with any mutual contacts. The type of material you are looking for includes:

- Previous companies they have worked for.
- Their experience and achievements.
- Any commonalities you may have, including mutual acquaintances.
- An indication of their preferred communication style.
- A pointer to their values and what matters to them.
- Any publications or other material they have put in the public domain.

By finding out about the person, you are achieving a number of things:

- You have the material for an icebreaker or "small talk" prior to address-ing the substantial content of the meeting. By doing this you create the chance for the person to relate to you.

- You signal the importance of the person. Dale Carnegie, the author of *How to Win Friends and Influence People*,[6] thought that the desire to feel importance was "the big secret" to getting on with people. This in turn builds trust and your ability to influence the interaction.

- You gain insight into how they prefer to communicate. Are they detail- or people-oriented, theorists, or action-oriented? You can then tailor your style to be effective.

- You gain a sense of their motivation. With this you can direct your communication towards not only what you can do – which may help them – but also link this to what really matters to them.

- You find out what you have in common. This helps both of you to feel comfortable and to establish a "fit" between you and your client.

- You speed up all the interpersonal analysis that you would otherwise be doing during the meeting, giving you a running start in the meeting.

Meeting

Eventually, it is time to meet with your contact. The initial meeting can be the make-or-break step in the sales process. It may be the first time that both parties get the opportunity to size each other up and determine whether a personal and commercial relationship (which may last years) is agreeable. The main objectives of the meeting are:

1 To start to build trust and to find out about each other.

2 To explore the situation, issues, or requirements that the contact may have (the needs).

---

[6] Carnegie, D. (2006). *How to Win Friends and Influence People*. Random House UK Ltd. p. 19. (First published in 1936.)

3 To establish any possible match between the services that you offer and the apparent needs, and to work out how to gather further information if that match is not yet clear.

4 To agree the next steps.

Start to Build Trust

The initial meeting is really a microcosm of how any future working relationship would develop. Both parties are looking to see how communication works, and if there is a spark. Values are being shared and cultural fit determined.

The first meeting is therefore a major chance to develop trust. The parties are looking at trust in two ways – the personal element and the professional. The concept of personal trust revolves around such questions as – How do I feel about this person? Do I get along with them? Can I believe them? Do I feel that they have my best interests at heart? Professional trust, on the other hand, focuses on how one party perceives the professional capability of the other, and whether they have confidence in what the other claims they can do.

Once the meeting begins, it is important to have an agenda to achieve your aims. Without this (or by allowing the client to run the agenda), you risk not achieving your objectives. A simple agenda can follow the objectives outlined above, where you cover problem exploration, motivations and fears, need and service matching, and next steps.

Explore the Situation

The major objective of the meeting is to explore the situation which brought you and your contact together. Fundamentally, the basic interaction of consultants and client is as follows:

Consultants are there to fulfil a need that clients cannot meet (or always meet) by themselves. Needs are the reason why clients engage consultants. This is typically a problem to be solved or a resource request to be filled. Needs can sometimes be explicit and easy to recognise, or implicit, hidden, or vague. Mostly needs are driven by the client. On occasion, needs can be created by a consultant identifying both a problem and a solution.

Problems and issues can drive need. If solving the issue is beyond the experience or capability of an organisation to solve on their own, then they may engage a consultant who has the appropriate skillset.

Requirements can also drive need. A requirement may result from a project or other organisational change where change is the process of moving from one current state to a second (improved) state.

In his book *The Introvert's Edge*, Matthew Pollard[7] advises using four questions to derive the client's needs:

- What do they want?
- What are they doing about it right now ... and is it working?
- Who says it is a problem?
- What is it costing them financially – in opportunities and/or personally?

This part of the meeting focuses on listening and clarifying. Where meaning is not clear or language is opaque, clarify before moving on. It should also focus on trying to understand the client's motivations and any fears they may have of engaging with you (see Chapter 1 – Clients: Emotions, Motivations, and Fears).

Establish a Potential Match

Only once enough fact-finding has been completed, move to the subject of possible solutions and how you might deliver any solutions. Even when this stage is reached, look for opportunities to begin a mutual exploration and craft a joint route. Putting the groundwork in at this early point, helps with any future solution development.

---

[7] Pollard, M. with Lewis, D. (2018).*The Introvert's Edge: How the quiet and shy can outsell anyone.* Amazon Books. p. 81. (First published in 1983.)

To demonstrate that you can meet a client's requirement, you need to gradually draw a picture for them. There are three aspects you need to demonstrate, and this process can be approached in a top-down manner:

- Your capabilities (services), which are relevant to the client and their requirements.
- Your credentials, which refer to your experience in these abilities.
- How you would apply this experience to the particular client's circumstances and requirements.

You are aiming to leave the other party with an impression of how quickly you grasped the problem, how much relevant experience you have, and how quickly you would hit the ground running.

Agree the Next Steps

At the very end of the meeting – if you feel there is a possible opportunity – it is wise to take the temperature of the other party by asking whether they, too, see an opportunity. If not, you have further work to do, so spend some time exploring what is required to get to this point. Unless the client accepts that there is a problem to solve or a need to be addressed, there is little chance of success.

In all circumstances, it is important to discuss and agree what the next actions are, based on the meeting. You may wish to qualify at this point (see below), or it may be that further investigation and subsequent discussion are necessary.

If further investigation is needed, plan to iterate through the cycle of investigation and discussion until the path forward is clear. During this time, continually focus on the potential match of need and service. You may have to collect additional information from the client themselves, from other people in the client organisation, or from your own contacts and organisation. Investigate whether you can tailor some of your services. Though, at this point, you are not creating the solution – that is the next stage and is part of the consulting rather than the sales process.

It is important to get the balance right between collecting information and asking things of the client, which can be onerous for them. A certain amount of persistence is necessary here, but too much contact may be overbearing and risk damaging the early relationship and trust.

Step 3 – Qualify the Opportunity

At various points during the iteration, and as a final part of the process, you should qualify the lead. Qualification is the process of understanding whether the consultant or consultancy is capable of and willing to provide a solution, and whether the consultant believes that the other party is sufficiently committed to the process. Put simply, is it worth the time and effort you need to commit for the potential benefit you may gain? There are a number of reasons why a consultancy may choose to **qualify out** of an opportunity. A lack of skills in the required areas, or a mismatch in timing, for instance. The work may be more hassle than it is worth (perhaps this is a client with a reputation for being difficult). Perhaps the work does not align with your strategy or values.

The following set of questions provides a good starting point to help you decide on how to qualify the opportunity. The answers will rarely be black and white, but taken as a whole, they will be indicative of the potential match of the parties and whether it is wise to pursue the opportunity further.

Qualification Questions

1 Is this the "real" client and are they empowered to make decisions?

2 What are the immediate opportunities?

3 What is the overall size of the opportunity in the long term?

4 What is the likelihood of converting the opportunity to paid work?

5 Is there budget to start?

6 Is there current or future potential to cross-sell (other services)?

7 Is there current or future potential to up-sell (other departments)?

8 Is there current or future potential to on-sell (next part of the cycle)?

9 How much effort is required to win? Is it a reasonable amount relative to potential opportunity and chances of winning? (The reasonable effort test).

10 Is there a sense of any resistance? Is this resistance likely to add to the effort to win?

11 Is there 50/50 participation? (Too much of an imbalance indicates a potential unequal relationship).

12 Is this work within core capabilities?

13 Is there the capability to deliver when the client wants?

14 Do I or we have experience of dealing with this client?

15 Does this work fit with the agreed consultancy strategy and plan?

16 Does this client have similar values to allow us to work together?

17 Will working with this client harm or enhance your reputation?

There is a high price to pay for poor qualification – significant amounts of wasted time. Given that most leads do not convert to opportunities and most opportunities do not result in business, the impact of not properly considering the situation before you can be considerable. It can also come with significant opportunity cost for those opportunities that may not get the attention they deserve.

A "no" from the client is absolutely fine. It is often better than continued uncertainty, and a "yes" is, of course, better still.

By the end of the Sales step, we either have an opportunity that can be explored in the Advise stage, or we have qualified out and no further effort is expended in this area at this time.

Contracting

During the Contracting step, you and the client finalise the agreement to work together. The proposed agreement is documented, reviewed, and signed. This may be a single document known as the proposal, or multiple documents, including the contract (sometimes known as the Statement of Work, Services Agreement, or Terms and Conditions).

The Contracting step has a dual objective: providing clarity on what has been agreed and providing a mechanism for enforcement should there be a future dispute around what was agreed.

Contracting is a recurring step that will repeat many times, not just after the initial pre-sales step, but each time further agreements are made with the client. For example, the initial sale may provide for you to perform some analysis, and after the analysis step, you may contract for the next step – recommendation activity. Or you may contract to provide recommendation for a system change and find that a further Contracting step is necessary prior to delivery of the recommended change.

Contracting is a not a step that should occupy you for long. It is advisable to initiate this step only when the deal is nearly done. If this is a stage that you find yourself in for too long, then it may be that you have entered this stage too early. In this case, it might be wise to force the issue to resolution (either positive or negative). You may discover that the client is not fully committed or motivated. In which case, it is better to discover this earlier rather than later, instead of wasting time and effort and risking the potential opportunity-cost of losing any other clearer opportunities.

Contracting is a step that needs to be entered into freely and with all actors understanding in full what has been committed to on both sides. Without this, future disharmony in relationship, or even legal contractual problems, are almost inevitable. Vague language, or surprises, or hidden terms should be avoided. Any arguments over specific areas have to be resolved before progressing. Protracted arguments may indicate something more fundamental is wrong and may even cause you to consider the viability of the engagement, even at this very late stage.

The initial contract is the place to set the expectations, not just for the topic currently under discussion, but for all interactions between you and the client in the future. In fact, the contract stage is the point of maximum leverage in the entire relationship. It is the most effective point for you, as a consultant, to set your expectations and the ground rules for your involvement. If any issues are identified, it is especially important not to avoid these because it sets precedent for all subsequent interactions. This can be much more difficult to recover from at a later point.

The detailed steps for contracting are:

1 Document your proposal.

2 Consider your pricing strategy.

3 Create your commercial agreement.

4 Sign off!

Document the Proposal

Once the decision has been made in principle to proceed, you need to document the agreement in a proposal and proactively press for sign off to ensure that the work performed so far results in a successful outcome.

The **proposal document** contains the solution or service that fits the client need. It is best to consider the proposal document only once the work has been agreed in principle. The alternative to this – to use the proposal as the agreement vehicle – may result in a long and inefficient final phase that ties up your energy and time. In keeping with the drive for efficiency, a proposal document should be kept short, focusing on just the elements related to the specific solution, and keeping away from less relevant material, such as company profiles or case studies.

The cost or price is a key element of any proposal, but when presented, should not come as a surprise at this point to the client. Instead, broad or ballpark costs should have been discussed earlier in the process to ensure that the client is comfortable in this area. Doing so allows you to judge the seriousness of the client before investing time, and it allows you to push back honestly should there be cost pressure. The proposal document includes a number of sections as detailed in the table below:

Section	Description
Requirements	You should provide a recap of the client need to demonstrate and check understanding.
Objectives	The goals of the proposed engagement should be specified. At the proposal stage, you will almost certainly not have all the information that would be uncovered during the engagement, so these objectives may be caveated.
Key Success Factors	How you and your client will judge the successful implementation. These factors may be in terms of activities completed, sign off achieved, or measurements to be targeted.
Scope	What will be delivered and what will not, including products, outcome activities, and deliverables.
Plan	The resourcing required to deliver the solution, as well as dates and a high-level plan.
Cost	The total cost for delivering the services and the breakdown of how the cost was calculated.
Benefits	The overall value of the investment to the client should the engagement be successful, including measurable and qualitative return on investment.
Client Provisions	Any assumptions and consultant needs, such as support or necessary information.
Follow Up	You may wish to include a proposal to follow up in order to judge success or make further change.

A certain amount of effort is required to ensure quality and relevance, and a proposal should be properly reviewed and proofread; however, a certain amount of efficiency is also necessary since a consultancy will typically be producing many proposals.

The proposal has to be well pitched. A successful proposal:

- Acknowledges and shows understanding of the client's problem.
- Demonstrates a detailed knowledge of how to approach the problem.
- Indicates implicitly or explicitly that you have solved this or similar problems before.
- Demonstrates control of timing and resourcing.
- Is pitched at the right level of detail for the client.

Once the client has received the proposal document, a process of revising the proposal to ensure it meets the need, may occur. As there has been agreement in principle, this should be limited. Timescales and cost are usually the elements that are scrutinised at this stage.

Statement of Work: Creating the Contract

Once the proposal is complete, you may need to create a **Statement of Work** or **Services Agreement**. These documents are the legal agreement (contract) that includes all the terms and conditions. The Services Agreement includes much the same as the proposal but is much more "finalised" and goes to a more detailed level to avoid any ambiguity. A Statement of Work might not always be needed, depending on how detailed the proposal was, or you may choose to combine the two if having both documents risks prolonging or confusing the process.

A Statement of Work will typically include:

- **Solution.** A high-level description of all elements of the solution, including the inputs and the interrelationships of the elements. Include the benefit and how this addresses the need.

- **Deliverables.** This may vary from individual items, such as documents and products, to entire outcomes.

- **Cost.** The total cost to deliver the solution and deliverables, broken down so that the calculation is clear.

- **Timescale.** Any key dates agreed to by both parties, such as product delivery dates, and how long resources will be assigned.

- **Key personnel.** Any named key personnel, with roles and responsibilities.

- **Terms and conditions.** Including working hours, payment terms, terminations, IP, confidentiality, dispute processes. You should strive to keep terms short to reduce the review difficulty, but not so short as to add unacceptable risk.

If you are creating your own terms and conditions, you have control over what you wish to include. The other party may wish to make amendments and you will need to decide whether the request is acceptable or provides too much risk. In any event, you are in control of the process, and you can ultimately say yes or no to the request. It may be requested that you use the other party's terms and conditions. Again, this is your choice. However, if you do accept this, take care to review the terms so that they are fair and contain an appropriate amount of risk. A checklist can therefore be useful. The table below provides a starting point for either constructing your own terms or reviewing another party's. At some point, however, you will absolutely need to consult a legal expert to ensure that the terms and conditions comply with the country's commercial law.

Area	Check
	Rates are clear and can be revised annually in line with CPI.
	Payment terms are 20 days after the month.
	Discounts are only applied in the event of prompt payment.
	Are expenses included?
Payment Terms	Overtime arrangement for additional hours, weekends, and public holidays.
	Is it clear what the arrangements are in the event of a delay to client deliveries?
	Right of interest for late payment.
Mutuality	Termination period is acceptable and mutual.
Insurance	Are the insurance thresholds valid?
	There is a limitation of liability of $5 million or less.
	Is there a non-solicitation clause?
Employee Matters	Right of substitution in the event of leave or resignation is included.
	Working hours are reasonable.
	Time approval processes.

Area	Check
Working Relationships	Performance deficiency, escalation, and dispute processes are included.
	Official communication is in writing and not verbal.
	Regular meetings with senior management (C-level and general management level) are included.
Intellectual Property	IP of either party is recognised as theirs and jointly created IP is recognised as belonging to both parties.
Confidentiality	There is a mutual clause of confidentiality.
Publicity	Client will provide the right for notification through social media and on the website that the companies are working together.
	Both companies agree to provide a reference or case study, assuming no disputes are in progress.

Consider your Pricing Strategy

Cost is a pre-eminent consideration during the Contracting step. For consulting, price is linked with subjective considerations regarding perceived and actual value, as well as with short- and long-term demand and supply considerations. The people-focused nature of consultancy, along with its inherent product, deliverable, and outcome variability, means that setting a price is rarely straightforward.

When setting your initial pricing during the early part of building a relationship with a new client, you will need to have a strategy that balances value for the client with commercial acceptability for yourself, all the while giving yourself the best chances of landing the deal. You should factor in the following considerations:

- **Timing.** The time to talk price is when the value is clear to the customer. Consulting services are not cheap, and price without context often comes as a shock to even experienced clients.

- **Market-based pricing.** This is where you price your services in line with current prices for similar services in the market. This is easy to justify, and client decisions then come down to perceptions of relative value between you and other consultants or service providers.

- **Cost-based pricing.** This is where you price using the margin of profit. Here you calculate the price using a calculation of the cost of providing the service, with an acceptable margin added to cover additional costs of running the business and providing a profit. A typical margin for a consultancy might be 35%.

- **Value-based pricing.** This is where price is set based on a percentage of the perceived benefit. For example, using a 10% value basis, if the value delivered to the client is $1 million, then the fee would be $100,000.

- **Price maximisation.** In order to maximise price, you may wish to start high and be prepared to be negotiated down. This can be done to maximise price, but it carries a higher risk of not winning the work. This is more suitable for when demand outstrips supply in the market.

- **Rate card.** A rate card is a list of your services with the price to the client. This has the advantage of setting expectations but the disadvantage of potentially losing commercial flexibility. In addition, a rate card breaks the link between price and value as it is typically free of important context.

- **Quality guarantee.** If the client is uncertain, you may try a guarantee. This has two forms: offering an investment engagement (for example, free of charge or at cost), or a guarantee of no charge in the event of the client not being satisfied.

- **Fixed pricing.** The price is a set figure, irrespective of the effort or timescales. This can provide certainty for the customer and incentive for the consultant to find efficiencies to minimise the effort involved. This comes with risk, however, and you need to have some elements in the contract that triggers a change if needed.

- **Capped pricing.** Capped pricing also provides a level of certainty for the client but has the added advantage of potentially coming in at a lower cost if the delivery is quicker or less effort than planned for. This is quite an attractive proposition, but with little upside for the consultant.

- **Discounts.** From time to time, you may wish to offer, or clients may request, a discount as part of the contract. Examples are bulk or long-term discounts. If you are happy to provide a discount (and this may be valid to maximise your chances of winning the work), it is important to do so carefully and in a controlled manner so that you are not locked into a long-term commercially disadvantageous position. When discounting, therefore, do so in a clear and finite way to ensure that the perception of the value you are providing is not compromised.

- **Value-add.** An alternative strategy to discounting, which can be used instead of or alongside, is increasing value-add. Value-add is the concept of providing additional benefits for no additional cost. This means the overall value of the service is increased in the minds of the client while your revenue is not diminished. Generic value-add types include education/training, investment services (free or low-price services that benefit both parties), access to your formal or informal knowledge base, access to other experts in your company or your network, or access to your IP and innovations.

Sign Off for Clear Agreement and to Press Forward

When there is no longer any debate about the content of the contractual document or the agreement to go forward, the consultant then presses ahead to ensure the document is signed and countersigned. If earlier qualification is effectively performed and the signing authority is both identified and aligned, then this process will go smoothly.

Problems may, however, occur even at this last stage:

- Sign off delays mean the agreed start date is passed.
- Lack of signing authority from the client indicates that they may not have buy-in from within their organisation.
- A disagreement may arise around specific terms and conditions.
- There are additional client financial hurdles, such as the need for a purchase order number.

A fully executed contract has the signatures of both parties and any related processing done at both ends, such as purchase order creation and communication.

It is possible to go ahead without full execution of the contract and many engagements do. This has the benefit (sometimes) of the consultancy being able to engage earlier, but this needs to be weighed against:

- The risk of sign off not happening and payment being withheld.
- Key terms and conditions not being enforceable, such as IP ownership (this is a risk for both parties).
- Continued negotiations, even though work has started, taking focus away from delivery and creating reduced leverage for you.

Once you have sign off ... Congratulations! Now the real work begins – delivering on your commitment.

3

ADVISE

| Analyse | Design | Validate |

Figure 8.   The Consultant's Playbook Structure – Advise Steps and Activities

In this chapter you will read about the Advise stage. This is a three-step consulting process which takes up after the initial Contracting step. You will learn about deriving true need through analysis activities, designing potential solutions, and validating these with the client.

The Advise and Act Stages

All the work done so far – marketing, selling, and contracting – will hopefully bring you to this, the chance to deliver your services. And whatever your specific skills and services, most of the time, you will perform at least one of the following high-level activities for clients:

1   **Analysis.** You are taking data, studying and understanding it to gain insight and form a conclusion about what that data reveals, focusing on what the client needs, whether it be a problem that requires solving or an opportunity that is to be pursued.

2   **Recommendations.** You are suggesting a way forward that will have positive benefits for the client and meet the client's need.

3   **Change.** You are implementing or forming part of a team that implements a solution to meet the client's need.

The actions that you would perform for each of these activities are therefore different. As a consultant, you should be ready to perform well in any of these situations.

The next two chapters are devoted to documenting the Advise and Act stages, and all the activities that these major scenarios encompass. The Advise and the Act stages together form a full Delivery Process, with Advise focusing on analysis and recommendation, and Act focusing on change. Specifically, the analysis activity maps to the Analyse step of the process. The recommendation activity is performed by the Design and Validate steps, and the change activity is covered in the Initiate, Solutions Delivery, and End steps of the process.

To help you remember this, the first letters of each of the steps within the Advise and Act stages spell out the acronym ADVISE – **A**nalyse, **D**esign, **V**alidate, **I**nitiate, **S**olutions Delivery, **E**nd.

Sometimes, for a given engagement with a client, these steps occur in logical sequence, and you moving through them all after the Acquire activities. In such a case, you may only contract once, immediately after the pre-sales stage. In other cases, you may need to perform each step individually, contracting the next element at the end of every preceding step. Either option is common in cases where the work is part of one initiative, and later steps are dependent on earlier ones.

Equally common is moving on to a new piece of work with the same client. Here you may perform the same step, multiple times. For example, making multiple recommendations and iterating multiple times through the Analyse, Design and Validate steps, for separate projects. In this case you would re-enter from the Acquire process, contracting each time.

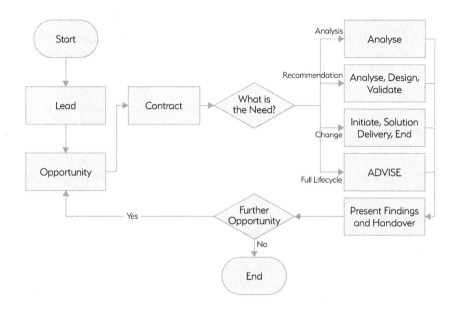

Figure 9. The Advise Process Flow

Analyse

By the time you enter the Analyse step, there is both consultant and client go-ahead to look for a solution to meet a need, and from a sales perspective, there is an opportunity that has been qualified. At this point, more in-depth investigation is required so that you can develop a fuller understanding of the need. Then you can clearly articulate back to the client your understanding of what they wish to achieve, before potentially moving on to the later stages of Design and Validate. The objective of the Analyse step is, therefore, to progress from an articulated perceived need to deriving the client's "true need".

The client's stated need can sometimes be explicit and easy to recognise, and at other times implicit, hidden, or vague. Any explicitly stated need should only be seen as the starting point in any discussion undertaken in an attempt to derive the true need. This true need can be hidden for a number of reasons. Clients may not themselves have a full picture or be equipped to see any further than the visible manifestation of a more complex problem. They may not yet trust you with all the information, or they may have as yet unknown reasons for not disclosing certain things.

Once this true need is found, you should bring it into the open so that any decision to move forward to a solution is based on the true need. Any assignment risks not being successful unless the true need is found and responded to.

During this process, you may discover a number of wide-ranging issues or organisational needs. But not all needs need to be responded to. You are not there to solve every problem and may not be equipped to provide solutions for everything, so this activity is just as much about scoping out and scoping in.

Whilst much of the groundwork has been done in the previous Acquire stage, the scope and depth of the activities in this step are considerably increased, and you may decide to charge a fee for the work. Only in the simplest of situations is most of the effort already completed.

True need is derived by performing three activities in which you:

- **Connect** with other parties who can provide additional information and help you clarify by performing further interviews, reviewing documents, and collecting data.
- **Challenge** the client on the stated need and the status quo.
- **Categorise** your findings for feeding into subsequent steps.

At the end of this stage are further optional steps, depending on the scope of the existing engagement and commercial agreement:

- Presenting findings.
- Reworking.
- Contracting for further engagements.

Connect

In any engagement you will have a number of opportunities to clarify the client need. The first opportunity for this was in the Sales stage, but it is in the Advise stage where you really begin to widen the enquiries, often including into your discussions people in the client organisation other than the initial contact. The objective here is to **clarify** your understanding of the client situation by performing activities which establish further details. This includes why the requirement has come about, who the customer is, what the expected timelines are, and whether there are any key constraints, such as budgetary constraints. Whilst this step can be seen as an iterative process, it is important to note that a client's time is valuable, and any questioning should be efficient.

To this point, you may have only engaged with one person or perhaps a limited group. This has provided general direction and a feel for the need, but one person's view is just that – the view of only a single person. To perform a thorough and complete analysis, you need to connect with and take input from others within the client organisation. This performs the dual task of getting closer to understanding the true need and developing necessary relationships that foster buy-in, which any subsequent successful change requires.

Your aim should be to identify and meet with a range of other stakeholders to help you build out your understanding derived from the Sales step. These stakeholders should represent a wide cross section of viewpoints to provide diversity of input. Without this, there are the risks of generalising the situation from a small cross section and missing vital information.

The starting point to identifying individuals is to ask the original contact to provide their names. They may mention their own manager, who will at least be interested or possibly responsible for the relationship with you. You need to identify this **senior client** and attempt to build relationships with them, and extract information from them, too. You also need to consider the **financial client**, the person who authorises the spend and who pays the bills, if this is not a previously identified party. This is particularly important since many valid opportunities to consult fail to get authorisation because funding is not considered until too late in the process. During conversations in which other client parties are mentioned, you should be seeking insights and, if necessary, querying whether it would be beneficial to contact them.

Your own experience of similar engagements can help you to identify people in important or useful roles across teams, programmes, or the client organisation, who ought to be consulted. Complexity arises when these clients have different or opposing agendas. As a consultant, it is your job to surface, acknowledge, and help deal with these conflicts, often in a way that achieves consensual outcome or at least moves any conflict to a decision point.

Clarify with Interviews

The purpose of identifying a wide range of contacts is to gather information from a broad pool. An interview with each is the next necessary step. In a fundamental way, the real value in consultancy is in this interaction between consultant and client. A client's time should be regarded as a finite resource (as is yours), and it is important to use the time efficiently. Adhering to the following principles will help in this regard. Interviews should be purposeful – with that purpose communicated in advance, time-bound and structured, recorded and the notes shared, respectful of the client, mostly listening and not talking, and summarised for clarity.

Much as is the case during the Sales step, it is important to have an agenda to achieve your aims and ensure that the person you are meeting is clear on the process and objectives of the session. The following structure may help provide the basis for any interview:

1 Welcome and small talk

2 Introduction with context and structure

3 Main interview

4 Summary of what has been discussed and captured

5 Next steps

6 Post-interview activities

It is the third step, the main interview, where the bulk of the focus should lie. A combination of high-level questions and questioning techniques should be used to help build out your understanding of the client's true need.

You can consider using the same questions as you asked the original contact:

- What do they want?
- What are they doing about it right now ... and is it working?
- Who says it is a problem?
- What is it costing them financially – in opportunities and/or personally?

In addition, the following four techniques are useful in helping to derive true need. A consultant should consider using one or all of these in their discussions with clients. A brief description of each appears next:

- **Appreciative enquiry** is all about making enquiries to find the core positives of an organisation. Once identified, you can consider the strengths and the possibility of using these as part of the solution. The client's true need must acknowledge and incorporate previous success, and any change needs to recognise what should remain the same.

- **Root-cause analysis** is a technique for identifying the root causes of a problem. It attempts to answer the following compound question: What is the problem, why did it happen, and how can we prevent it happening again? It encourages in-depth analysis to understand the whole system and the possible multiple causes of a problem.

- **Powerful questions** are thought-provoking queries that are often successful in establishing truth. These are often used by professional coaches to encourage deeper thought and eliminate evasion. Over time, you can compile your own list of powerful questions that can be used with multiple clients.

- **Five whys** is a simple root-cause analysis technique which involves asking why a problem occurred in an iterative manner, with each successive why question based on the answer to the previous one. By the time the question has been asked five times, the cause of an issue and a solution should have been identified.

Clarify by Collecting Other Data

Besides individuals, there are a number of other primary sources of information you can use once you have identified and interviewed the various client parties. These are client data, internal (your own) data, and external data, which should all be collected and considered.

Client data includes documents, presentations, videos, and other recorded sources. The type of client data and documents you require depends on the nature of the project. You need to ask the client for access to any relevant documents or material that might help your understanding. As a general statement, however, the following typical document types might help:

- Business cases
- Requirements specifications
- Problem statements
- Business plans or departmental plans
- Quarterly or annual reports
- Client market and competitor analysis
- Organisational structure
- Values, mission or vision statements

Internal data is your education, history, and knowledge of previous assignments – specifically their results and relevant good and bad experiences. This, combined with colleague and contact experiences, is a rich source of information to be mined and is, of course, your generic value proposition as an expert consultant. The questions that need asking and answering for every assignment are:

- Have I or any of my colleagues done something similar before?
- How did it go?
- Was it successful?
- Is there anything I can reuse?
- What was learned and how would I improve it?

To be truly effective, this internal data should be captured and catalogued within a knowledge management system, as informal systems (or memory) are not always sufficiently robust for taking experience from one client to another.

External data takes the concept of mining your own experience further when you widen this out to questioning of external sources. Industry or domain literature and external knowledge repositories can be interrogated for suitable frameworks or existing analysis of similar situations. Examples of valuable external sources include:

- Analyst organisations, such as Gartner and Forrester.
- Investment analysts, who analyse company and market sector performance.
- Specific industry or domain organisations.
- International standard organisations.
- Google!

Clarify by Other Sources

Questionnaires are another method to source client data. Online software has made surveys extremely easy to create and distribute. However, the design of questionnaires is important to achieve objectivity and avoid ambiguity and leading questions.

Some rules for questionnaires include:

- Have a defined and considered distribution list, not a scattergun approach.
- Have a clear and transparent purpose.
- Keep it short enough for respondents to complete without inconvenience.
- Use language that is logical, clear, simple, and unambiguous.

Survey responses are rarely answered by all and often require follow up. Respondents, therefore, tend to be those who have something to say and may veer to the extreme. Again, generalising from survey responses risks being misleading, unless a high take-up has occurred, or outlier input is moderated.

In addition, those who have taken part in a survey are often interested to know the outcome. Consideration should be given to publishing summary findings. Where those canvassed are potentially affected by any change that the consultant is engaged in, sharing the findings has the additional benefit of deepening understanding and buy-in. In turn, this leads to more successful outcomes.

Observation is a process where the consultant works closely with and observes an individual or team to learn how things are done and how work is performed. This activity may be performed if there is a perceived problem generating the true need and the problem is "observable".

Observation is a method that can also be used for performance assessment, or for creating standard operating procedures. In consulting, you can use this to help visualise problems or to generate systems requirements. A good observation process follows a number of principles:

- It is explained beforehand.
- It should make people comfortable and not antagonised.
- It focuses on the problem at hand and does not get distracted.
- It is documented.
- It is always on the lookout for problems and gaps.

Care should be taken to mitigate for your own "observer bias", instances where the results of observations are influenced by your own expectations. For example, if you expect to see risky behaviour, then you are more likely to conclude that what you are observing is in fact risky.

Finally, **focus groups** and **workshops** have some advantages over interviews, with increased interactivity and a more natural environment. There are risks with this approach, including the possibility of louder voices prevailing or at the other extreme, a type of groupthink emerging. Design by committee is a real risk, too, with an excess of compromise leading to middle-of-the-road thoughts.

Challenge

The ability to **challenge** is one of the key value propositions of a consultant. Your independence, experience, and skills mean you are in an ideal position to professionally advocate positions other than the current understanding. This can occur in a number of ways.

First, you can **challenge the stated need** in order to arrive at a more precise or exact need. This is in essence what you will have begun to do through your clarification activities and will continue to do through the Design and Validate steps to come.

Second, you can **challenge the status quo** by proactively suggesting enhancements to promote change. You can use your experience, expertise, and your intellectual property to suggest improvements or alternative interpretations to what the client sees. "Consultant-led" needs such as this can be created by identifying both a problem and a potential solution for a client, though care must be taken not to simply identify a solution without a real need being present. Challenging the status quo can be approached in two ways:

- When you are not particularly knowledgeable about the client but have worked in similar situations or with similar clients, then you may be able to make suggestions and see what resonates with the client and is therefore worthy of further discussion.

- When you do have knowledge or experience, then you can take a more precise approach, suggesting and recommending an action or measure that you feel will have specific benefit for the client.

Third, you must **challenge collusive requests.** In this situation, collusion is a secret or unspoken agreement between the client and the consultant. The conditions for collusion in the client–consultant relationship occur when the stated needs of the client are at odds with the real needs of the wider client organisation, and you act in line with this analysis. Collusion might take the following forms:

- When the client wants you to champion a point of view in order to meet a political goal.

- When they want you to recommend or deliver something that will not benefit the organisation but will benefit the individual.

- When they ask you to change information or hide information from other key stakeholders.

As well as ethically suspect, collusion will inevitably lead to poor solutions, and change failure. This in turn damages both client and consultant.

Categorise

Through clarification and challenge, you can derive the true need, which can then be classified. Richard Newton, in his book *The Management Consultant*,[8] suggests that all needs can be categorised as one of the following six question that a client is trying to answer:

- **Am I doing the right things?** Here the client is concerned with matters of strategy and direction. The consultant may need to consider the creation of strategies or conduct competitor or market analyses in order to meet these needs.

- **Am I doing things right?** This question indicates concern with operational or efficiency matters. They may wish to engage in a review of current processes or a benchmarking exercise to compare themselves to others.

- **How can I change to do things in the right way?** The client is looking for options for solutions and recommendations. The consultant may be thinking of analysis and design-type activities to achieve the necessary outcome.

- **How do I achieve the changes required?** It is likely that the client needs advising on the creation or implementation of plans, as well as specific processes to help implementation.

- **How do I implement the change plan I have?** The client needs advice on how to deliver a project, programme, or other change, or help with doing so.

---

[8]   Newton, R. (2010). *The Management Consultant: Mastering the art of consultancy*. FT Prentice Hall. p. 92.

- **What can I learn from what I have done?** Finally, the client may need help to review something that has been completed. Audits, performance reviews, or health checks may be appropriate services in this instance.

The activity of categorising is useful for the following reasons:

- First, it helps you understand where in the change lifecycle the client is, with the earlier questions relevant to early parts of the lifecycle.

- Second, it primes you to think about what consultant service might be relevant and may form part of the solution.

- Third, by labelling the problem, you are indicating that you have seen this before, helping the client gain confidence in your ability to propose the right solution.

- Fourth, by categorising, you can challenge more effectively. For example, "I don't think your problem is one of strategy, rather one of planning."

Positioning and labelling the problem as one of these question, helps you reduce the issue to one of simple language, which in turn leads to clarity of need and therefore accuracy of solution.

Present your Findings

Before you move to the next step, which focuses on designing potential solutions, you may wish to present your findings. Presentations are a common element of consultancy work. A presentation at this point is not as complex and demanding as that expected during the later Validate step, though it may be equally as important to both yourself and the client.

It may not be necessary to formally present at this point, since the analysis done so far may be your own internal stage as part of recommending a range of solutions. But there are several benefits to doing so, irrespective of the contractual requirements or the agreed outcome.

Presentation at this point allows:

- Firming of ideas, by enforcing structural thinking in order to present a clear narrative.

- Confirmation that your understanding is correct by replaying it back to the client.

- The client to gain further confidence in you, and potentially, confidence in your capability and suitability for continuing with the next stages.

- The client to "come on the journey" at the same time and speed as the consultant.

A suggested format for presenting analysis findings (without a proposed solution) is as follows:

Section	Details
Introduction	A simple introduction may include a history of how the parties were engaged and the format (contents) of the presentation.
Problem Statement	A description of the need that was presented, and the true need derived from the analysis activities. The problem statement(s) can also be categorised, using the six categories.
Market Analysis	Market analysis can be divided into two types: information from your own knowledge base, and information from external knowledge bases.
Data and Trend Analysis	If your information is data heavy, you may wish to add specific data (current) and trend (historical) analysis.
Implications and Opportunities	An "Implications" slide provides a projection of what will happen, given the problem and market analysis, should trends continue and no action be taken. Conversely, by taking action, there is opportunity, and the associated potential benefits can be highlighted.
Next Steps	A recommendation of the next steps to be taken in an effort to gain client agreement to maintain momentum towards positive action.

A well-delivered and well-received presentation will springboard you into either a successful contracting or design activity, or alternatively, will allow you to redirect or pivot without further wasted investment.

Contract for Further Engagement

If the initial contract or agreement has expired or does not cover further scope, and you are planning to continue to engage for additional activities, you will need to go through the contracting activity once more. The purpose of contracting at this point is to gather further buy-in and agreement to go to the remaining stages of designing and validation of the proposed solution. The steps are the same, but with a different focus. This is the second point at which you may need to go through the contracting phase, the first being during the initial Sales step and documented in the Acquire stage.

When documenting your proposal here, you will be documenting how you propose to deliver the solution. It is also useful to reference the work performed so far (though not in too much detail) to demonstrate continuity and to ensure that other stakeholders who may not have this detail are aware of it.

When considering your pricing strategy, ensure that you are consistent with previous rate cards and that the pricing strategy is similar. Though the pricing strategy does not need to be identical, it can be detrimental to surprise the client with an entirely different way of pricing if this has not been discussed earlier. The "feel" of the negotiation should therefore be the same. You may have also "discounted to win" during earlier contracting, but you may now be inclined to consider that you have proved your credentials and that there is more buy-in from the client. Consequently, you may be less likely or willing to continue with lower costing.

Considering the contract, it is likely that your terms and conditions will be the same, and it is probably wise in that any time terms and conditions get changed, there is additional review time and effort required from either party. Hopefully, any sign off processes are now fully understood by both parties, and the sign off is an efficient affair.

Design

During the Analyse step, you have developed a much better understanding of what the client truly needs, through a rigorous process of collecting data, challenging, and categorising. This knowledge should now be used to begin the process of creating solutions to match the need.

The objective of the Design step is to identify and outline potential solutions. Through a process of generating ideas, validating, and organising them, a small number of options are prioritised for further discussion with the client. This process usually involves balancing the efficiency of using existing services (which may be yours or others) with the need for tailoring to match more closely the exact need that has been identified. Too little tailoring can lead to solutions which are not fit for purpose, whereas too much can lead to unnecessary cost and time expended.

Good design also involves the client and consultant participating in joint solution creation. This increases the likelihood of an acceptable solution, which in turn leads to sustained improvement once the solution is implemented. The design activity therefore includes "testing the water" and regular communication as key success factors.

You now need to organise your data so that options can be chosen and presented to the client, along with a recommendation, to ensure that the client is fully empowered to make a decision during the Validate step (and not you, the consultant). The following activities are part of the Design step:

- Create the longlist.
- Match options to create solutions.
- Craft a joint solution.
- Create the shortlist.
- Check that the options are valid.

Create your Longlist

Once there is enough information, a likely range of solutions will present themselves, while others will eliminate themselves. This is the process of longlisting, that is, creating a large number of options that you later pare back into a shortlist. Although you may have an early preference at this time, you should continue to go through this activity and ensure that you generate less obvious solutions, even if you later discard them. Also incorporate any preferred client-options (even if you later discard them).

Methods to build your longlist include:

- **Using prior experience.** Use your own experience of previous solutions. After all, part of your value proposition is your experience in previous similar situations.
- **Using others' experience.** Ask other colleagues or contacts for their previous exposure to similar problems and how they handled them.
- **Using client experience.** Include client preferences and ideas because clients may have done their own research and may also be quite highly educated in the area.
- **Brainstorming.** This is the technique of rapidly noting down ideas without spending time in assessing their suitability, with the aim of stimulating lateral thinking and sparking creative solutions.
- **Research.** Use your own and publically available knowledge bases in order to collect previously created solutions to the problem.

By the end of this step, you may have anything between three and ten or more potentials.

During this stage, there may be a chance to test the water with some of the solutions, remembering again that a client's time is valuable.

If there are no credible options available, or it is thought that no option is likely to be palatable, then an early meeting to present this finding is necessary, rather than going to the Validate step.

Match Options to your Services to Create Solutions

A solution is the specific and tailored matching of a service with a need. A quality solution relates to actual need. A solution which does not relate to the problem is not really a solution. It is easiest to meet a need with a service, but a generic service may not be the best solution.

If your service matches your potential solutions, then this is a very simple exercise. Your solution *is* your service.

If your service nearly matches your solution, then you need to consider how to tailor the service so that it matches the solution. The general consultant value proposition is that of adding value. Tailoring services is an obvious example of value that has been added by an expert, and in a way that may not be possible by selecting a generic service. If you are to tailor a service, then you should consider how much tailoring is possible or desirable. The 80/20 rule sits well here. Services should be tailored on an 80/20 basis – with 80% being unchanged and 20% being different, unique, or new.

If your services require significant tailoring (more than 20%), then approach this with caution. Too much tailoring risks taking you away from your overall strategy and core capability and may affect your profit margins unless properly controlled.

A Note on Services, Solutions, and Outcomes

Three terms should be distinguished at this point. At first glance they may appear similar and are sometimes used interchangeably. Whilst they are all something that the client receives, the distinctions are important. The definitions are as follows:

- A **service** is something that the consultant provides. It is the set of visible activities and steps that are performed.
- A **solution** is the specific and tailored matching of a service to a need.
- An **outcome** is the effect of implementing the solution.

For your own purposes, there is a logical link between the terms. A service is tailored to create a solution, and a solution is designed to achieve an outcome. In turn, the outcome should always be in part to match the client need. This is important because when talking with the client, you should always bring the conversation back to the outcome and whether it matches the true need. Indeed, as clients become more experienced, there is a trend towards more outcome-based engagements where consultants are expected to have "skin in the game" (where a consultant takes additional risk for additional reward), helping to increase the likelihood of the outcome being achieved.

Craft a Joint Solution

A good time to begin to involve the client in helping to generate potential solutions is during the Design step. The concept of a joint solution rather than a consultant-driven one, and the inherent benefits attached, should be promoted to the client. Solutions are far more effective where client and consultant are both bought in, and a 50–50 partnership of equals has developed. Jointly creating solutions really helps drive towards this aim.

The benefits of jointly creating solutions include:

- Buy-in and increased confidence from the client.
- Improved relationships between the parties.
- An understanding how working with the client during the main delivery might go.
- Reduced client fears about engaging with you.

On the other hand, if you do not adhere to this principle, you risk:

- Imposing or trying to impose something not wanted.
- A consequent reduction in trust.
- Failure to achieve the potential benefits.

One way you might encourage this joint approach without formally presenting the options (which may not be ready at this stage), is by "testing the water". You do this by informally introducing an idea and judging the client's reaction. This can be done with a simple line such as "One idea I was considering ..." or "Something that is prevalent in the market at the moment is ...". This furthers the idea of a partnership between you and the client and reduces the chance of a potentially embarrassing misalignment (or at least, wasted time).

Although this activity is placed within the Design step, crafting joint solutions is really a principle that needs to be considered throughout the consulting lifecycle.

Shortlist so as Not to Overwhelm the Client

The activity of consulting is fundamentally that of giving advice to other people, and there are good and bad ways to do this. One of the more effective ways is to provide a limited set of options along with your recommendation, rather than only one or too many. This is because giving only one choice or recommendation may leave the client feeling that a decision is being made on their behalf. Your ability to be accepted as a trustworthy guide can be damaged if your client believes that you have already reached your own conclusion. On the other hand, giving too many choices, may lead to "choice overload". Choice overload results when having too many options makes it *more* difficult for the client to decide. Faced with too many choices, people tend to worry that they may make the wrong decision, and they are more likely to be dissatisfied after having decided. The result is that they often make *no decision at all*. This is less than optimum in the client–consultancy relationship.

Having understood this principle, it is at this point you need to make your longlist into a shortlist. If you have more time available, you may wish to perform your shortlisting after the validation is performed (the next step). If you are short on time, then you may need to validate on a cut-down version.

The following general critera can be used to reduce the longlist to a shortlist:

- Is the proposed option simple?
- Have you or your colleagues experience in delivering this solution?
- Is the cost likely to be acceptable?
- Is the implementation timescale likey to be acceptable?
- Does it meet the need?
- What level of risk is there with any potential implementation?

Ultimately, the choice of which solution to implement is the client's, not the consultant's. A solution imposed on a client will not find buy-in and will not work. The consultant will, however, wish to influence which solutions are implemented.

Check the Options are Valid

Finally, before presenting your shortlist of potential solutions to the client, add further detail for each option and check that each option to be presented is valid. Address each of the following questions to help you consider the suitability of the options on the shortlist:

- Have you confirmed it matches the need?
- Is it described in a clear and straightforward manner?
- Have you identified and documented the pros and cons of each option?
- Have you identified and documented key risks and a plan to mitigate them?
- Are the assumptions understood and documented?

Further questions are relevant, too, if you are the party likely to deliver the solution:

- Does it allow for your needs as a consultant? You have your own requirements to operate successfully as a business. Typical consultant's needs include:
  - Appropriate payment once the engagement is complete or perhaps at key milestones.
  - Approval for a case study or references so that you continue to build your profile and compile evidence of your capability.
  - Sponsorship into other business areas and higher up the organisation to build further relationships and potentially procure more work.
- Are the engagement needs identified? Since clients have access to things the consultant does not, they need to state that success is based on having this access, too. Moreover, clients have power, while consultants can only influence, so sponsorship and support are necessary. Typical engagement needs include:
  - Access to key project individuals.
  - Documentation.

- Space to work and appropriate equipment.
- Sponsorship and support.
- Project budget.
- Does it aid your own career goals? Like any professional, as a consultant, you will have your own personal career goals and motivations. This internal motivation and desire for meaningful work is quite distinct from business goals, such as the desire to successfully deliver and grow your business. Personal career goals and motivations include the need to:
  - Have your expertise better utilised.
  - Have your recommendations more frequently implemented.
  - Become more of a partner with your clients.
  - Avoid no-win consulting situations.
  - Develop internal commitment in your clients.
  - Receive support from your clients.
  - Increase your leverage.
  - Establish more trust between yourself and your clients.
- Finally, you should ask and answer the following important, fundamental question: Can you deliver?
  - Do you have the capability?
  - Do you have the skills?
  - Is this something you wish to deliver?

Validate

By the end of the Design step, you will have developed a range of solutions to present to the client. There may be an early favourite at this time, either because previous experiences inform you of its suitability, or because it was created during a period of joint solution-design. You now need to move to the next step – validating the options with the client.

The objective of the Validate step is to decide which of the potential solutions best meets the client's need.

During this step, the consultant goes through the process of outlining the options and the pros and cons of each, and then makes a recommendation. This recommendation can be written or delivered in person, with the decision primarily based on a client's preferences, rather than just the preferences of the consultancy.

The success of the Validate step, however, relies on successful preparation *before* the presentation. Determining your key messages and referring to these throughout the activity is critical, as is a cycle of draft, review, and practise to make sure the message is focused and slick.

The Validate step comprises the following activities:

- Preparing to present.
- Creating your presentation.
- Delivering the presentation.
- Reworking.
- Contracting.

Prepare to Present

The effectiveness of any presentation you deliver to a client is heavily influenced by the quality of the planning and preparation. This includes considering how best to present, who you are presenting to, the format of the interaction, and (if there are more than one of you) who will present.

Planning includes three key elements:

- Deciding on your key messages.
- Understanding who will be in attendance.
- Deciding on your presentation approach and team.

Decide on your Key Messages

Your key messages are the themes and ideas that you believe are most important to communicate and for your audience to understand. Considering these is the very first activity in presentation planning. Your key messages are important because they provide the direction for your presentation and the subsequent sanity check for quality. They also provide a common set of principles that everyone involved in creating the solution presentation can align to, and that the audience can understand and remember.

Key messages tend to focus on outcomes, value, and other reasons why the solution that you are proposing is the right one for the client. The messages, therefore, are highly situation dependent. Any of the following generic value types, though, may provide the basis for high-impact key messages:

1   **Innovation.** Your approach is up to date and innovative, and you keep your eye on developing trends so that you can bring these to your clients.

2   **Scalability.** The solution and services you provide will enable you to respond to peaks and troughs throughout the delivery.

3   **Industry recognised.** Your methods and solutions are recognised as successful throughout the industry or domain in which the client operates.

4   **Retains client knowledge.** You will retain existing knowledge by working it into the solution, both through formal and informal knowledge management methods.

5   **Capability.** You have the skills, experience, and knowledge to deliver this solution and that capability will be made available.

6   **Credentials.** You have a track record of success in delivering specific, similar, and relevant solutions.

7   **Measurable.** Through metrics and measurement, success can be quantified and monitored.

8   **Partnership.** You and the client will work together throughout, meaning continual communication, though you will take much of the client's burden on yourself.

9 Formalised. Your solution is formalised and recognised so that it is repeatable, scalable, and reliable.

10 Balanced. Your solution has the right balance of many of the above elements.

Understanding Who Will Be in Attendance

Another key activity in preparing for the presentation is to find out who you will be presenting to. Familiarise yourself with any drivers, motivations, and fears these individuals might have, as well as the roles they will play. Doing so will help you tailor your messages to better suit the audience. When looking at the roles that clients play, we identified in Chapter 1 that clients play one of the following role types: Authoriser, Owner, Gatekeeper, Key Influencer, Influencer, or Technical Buyer.

Within a presentation context, we can also add:

- The **Governor** who ensures that any decision meets internal guidelines or policies.

- The **Facilitator** who works between parties to provide options and solutions.

Deciding on the Presentation Approach

You may decide to present your options in either a written form or via a presentation – or you may be requested to use either of these methods. The choice of how you present will be heavily influenced by the client's preferred communication style, what the agreed process is, and your own strengths. If it is a written submission, then a high-quality document, which is well constructed and clear, is necessary. If it is verbal, then a clear presentation, using appropriate visuals, is necessary. Typically, both elements are pursued, that is, to deliver a face-to-face presentation but to leave the client with both a hard copy of the document and a digital version to consider in their own time. Whichever method – written, verbally presented or with elements of both – it is important to provide a high-quality presentation with just the right amount of information. A great solution can be destroyed by a poor presentation, or one that has too much or too little relevant information.

Assuming you are delivering a verbal presentation, practise and rehearsal is advisable. First impressions count, and the early-stage time with the client is the point at which trust can be heavily influenced. For both parties, this time will be indicative of the potential future working relationship.

You also need to decide on the presentation team. If you are a sole consultant, this decision is simple – it is you! But if you are part of a wider team, you should consider involving others, in particular, those who present well and are relevant in some way to the potential future engagement. In terms of attendees, roughly balanced client and consultant numbers are best.

When considering who forms part of your team, factors include:

1   Will the person add value? Do they have a specific role?

2   Does the person have a previous positive relationship with the client?

3   Will they present well? Do they look the part, and will they communicate well?

4   Does bringing the person send a key message, such as the importance of the client?

5   How does bringing the person reflect on the strengths and weaknesses of your team?

Create your Presentation

Once your planning is complete, you are ready to create your full presentation. Good planning will have made this step easier and the outcome better, too. There are three steps to this activity: creating the structure, creating the draft presentation, and dress rehearsal.

Step 1 – Create the Structure

The first step in building the presentation is to decide on a structure, that is, how to organise the content. The following structure can be used as a basis and is suitable for recommendation and option presentation types, which are the most common you will deliver as a consultant.

Section	Description
Contents	Structure and signposting are key principles for effective consultant presentations, and a single slide that outlines how the presentation will evolve, helps you organise the content and the flow of the presentation, allowing the audience to follow your path. In addition, the contents slide helps control the presentation by reducing upfront questions around content. Some consultants prefer to talk to the structure rather than creating a contents or agenda slide, but if your presentation is to be left as a document to read, having a contents slide may help.
Identified Need	This section needs to include a recap of the problems, requirements, or other needs that were initially presented to you. This prefaces the presentation for those who may not have been involved by creating context, and it demonstrates understanding and listening, and sets the scene for describing the analysis you performed.
Findings	Run through the analysis that you performed once you were presented with the initial need. This includes the process of how you arrived at your findings, and what the findings were. The true need that you identified should be clearly articulated, especially if it differs from the original stated need. It is useful to tell this in a story format, where each slide continues the argument from the previous slide.
Options	Work through each option you have analysed that meets the need, explaining: • Pros and cons • Potential costs (or at least scale of cost) • Timeline for implementation • Benefits of implementing the solution • Assumptions • Risks and mitigations • Your own needs and expectations

Section	Description
Recommendation	The recommendation should focus on the value where benefits are detailed and success is measurable. If you can apply a dollar amount, all the better. You also need to balance this message with realistic expectations, and it is rarely wise to guarantee outcomes.
Summary	Finally, you should recap the recommendation and the key messages. This embeds your presentation for your audience. Aim for three to five key points, which, if the audience remembered only this, would be effective in asserting your message.
Additional Slides – further information	At this end of the pack, you may decide to place certain slides that are not part of the central narrative, but which may provide more context, either for the audience to review afterwards or during question-and-answer time. These slides can also act as appendices where additional data that supports the major narrative can reside, when placing it in the main part of the presentation would affect the flow or distract from the message.

Step 2 – Create the Draft Presentation

Once the draft structure is complete, the details should be filled in to round out the presentation and create the first draft, which will provide the basis for subsequent improvement through iteration. The following generic principles are particularly relevant to consultant presentations:

- **Focus on your key messages.** These are the principles that you created earlier in this step. All content should underpin your themes. If a slide or a point within is not aligned to a key message, then it is probably superfluous and may be removed. Your key messages must be targeted at the planned audience, continually addressing the need. If this is not the case, then your key messages are incorrect or incomplete.

- **Be consistent.** Slides should look and feel consistent in structure and composition and not as if they were written by separate individuals, even if they were.

- **Be clear.** Contents slides, key messages, and summaries can all be used, as well as signposting on each page to indicate where the current slide is within the overall flow. Page numbers and section numbers help in this way.

- **Target your audience.** Your earlier investigation into your attendees will have given you a view of their preferred communication style. Your presentation needs to deliver something for everyone, without appearing mixed or contradictory.

- **Aim for "the right amount" of information.** This is true for each individual slide and the overall presentation. Comprehensiveness is not a goal and aiming for this distracts from the key messages and compromises clarity. Be concise and keep each slide to a small number of points, so as not to overwhelm. It is difficult for people to focus on more than three to five things at once.

- **Make it visually attractive.** Aim to break up text with diagrams and visuals. Visuals should add to the message, not just be there for attractiveness. Graphs or diagrams perform a dual role – they convey information and provide variation of appearance and arrangement.

- **Ensure it is professional.** This is a function of a number of elements, including appropriate branding, consistency of style, and appearing appropriately up to date. There is no shortcut here – keeping up with current stylistic trends in respect of colour, layout, and "feel" are necessary to make sure you do not look out of date.

Once a full draft is completed, it is important it undergoes a quality check process. You can use the following simple checklist to validate quality – you may wish someone independent to perform this verification.

Checklist - Presentation Quality

Criteria	Yes / No
Does it meet the need?	
Is it internally consistent?	
Is there a clear structure?	
Does the presentation relate a clear strategy?	
Are the key themes referenced and obvious?	
Is it free of errors and spelling mistakes?	
Are slides consistently formatted?	
Are there any sections which are too complex or too dull?	
Can it be delivered in the allocated time?	
Is it appropriately branded?	
Is there anything missing that should be included?	
Are there any obvious improvements to the presentation that others can see?	
Will the solution resonate with the intended audience?	
Is there a clear story that the audience can follow?	

Step 3 - Rehearse

Up to this point, everything has been focused on creating materials and documents for the presentation, but it is the delivery that will make the difference between success and failure. You need to practise running through the presentation in order to assess how well it fits together, and to familiarise yourself with the material. Aim for two or three practice runs for optimal preparation. The following hints and tips may help you:

- **Practise your introduction and conclusion.** If delivered well, these elements have an outsized bearing on the perception of your presentation. It is a quirk of the human mind to remember the start and the end of events more clearly than the middle. Learning these almost off by heart will allow you to ease into the presentation and be assured that your key messages are covered.

110

- **Practise out loud.** Get used to the sound of your own voice and make sure that any difficult-to-pronounce phrases are practised so that they are expressed without difficulty. This also gives your voice a work out, especially useful for more introverted or quiet types, for whom speaking requires focus and effort.

- **Get feedback.** Take feedback from people who have not seen the presentation before, as well as those who have been involved in its creation. This matches more closely the experience your final audience will have, and you will be able to see more accurately the impact of your delivery.

- **Make amendments after each iteration.** If slides do not match with your words, make amendments to one or the other, and repeat the section until it flows.

- **Time your presentation.** Ensure that it fits into the time allocated. It is most likely that you will have to remove rather than add material, though you may be able to reduce the time taken as a result of finding better, more concise ways to explain your points.

- **Make it a dress rehearsal.** As a final activity, perform a full, end-to-end run-through in conditions that are as close as possible to the arrangements for the day, sitting or standing as you plan to do in the real thing, and using the equipment you plan to use.

- **Answer potential questions.** Get someone to act as the client and have them ask relevant or potential questions. If this isn't possible, list potential areas where the client may ask for clarification or extra detail and try to produce two or three points that you would use to answer the question should it come up.

- **Video yourself.** Once you have got over the shock of how you sound, you will be able to take an objective view of how you look and sound when presenting, and then make the adjustments that are necessary.

With a successful rehearsal under your belt, you will go into the actual presentation feeling more confident, more practised, and more prepared for any difficult questions.

Present and Recommend
the Preferred Option for the Client

Once you are in the meeting, it is time to deliver your presentation. It is important that you look the part and feel ready. Here are three important tips for consideration in the few minutes just before meeting with the client or entering the presentation venue:

- **Check your dress and appearance.** You should dress appropriately for the situation, conveying a professional image. If in doubt, err on the side of smart. Good quality and well maintained are the key features for both yourself and your wardrobe! Do a final check on your personal presentation before entering to ensure you are well groomed.

- **Warm up your voice.** Talk to yourself in a mirror or even sing to get yourself used to your voice and to stabilise the volume and tone. You can carry on doing this by ensuring that you talk continually during any informal introductory period, such as when you enter the room.

- **Control nerves with breathing exercises.** The right amount of adrenaline can improve performance, but too much can weaken your voice or make you feel anxious. Breathing exercises help with both.

Once in the room, you should follow a straightforward process. A recommended format for a consulting presentation is as follows:

- **Greetings and introductions.** You should strive to make a good first impression. Do your best to project confidence and control as you enter. Introduce yourself and each team member. It is useful to explain why specific team members are present and why they might be relevant to the client or the proposal.

- **Deliver a recap.** Focus on the perceived need and a description of how this will be addressed in the upcoming presentation. Indicate how many options there are and describe each at the highest level.

- **Deliver a strong introduction.** This should include the structure of the presentation and the three to five key messages that you are hoping will resonate with the audience. These may form part of the presentation material, or you can decide to relay this information without any visual distraction.

- **Deliver the presentation.** Run through your prepared presentation keeping the following in mind:

  - **Project confidence.** Do so throughout the presentation. Adopt a good posture, look people in the eye, smile, and use open body-language. Strive for a controlled voice and try to eliminate verbal tics and hesitations.

  - **Divide your attention between the audience and the presentation.** Doing so demonstrates control of your material (and yourself) as well as providing personal contact. When focusing on the audience, make eye contact for a period of time that shows everyone respect but does not make people uncomfortable. Some people are less comfortable and may drop their eyes. Respect this and focus on others.

  - **Use intonation.** Intonation injects variety and interest. It also helps structure and clarity; with poor intonation, it can be difficult to understand where one point finishes and another starts.

  - **Know when to stop.** A good point makes itself; continuing with further elaboration may in fact dilute the impact and comprehensiveness is rarely a goal.

  - **Read the room.** Be aware of how the presentation is being perceived so you can react and adapt if necessary.

- **Questions and discussions.** The question-and-answer session is as important as the presentation. Whether you deal with questions as they come along or have a dedicated session at the end, at least half of the time available should be allotted to questions or discussion. In addition, you need to manage the questions to make sure that the direction of the session is not sabotaged, that no one hijacks the session, and that everyone on the client side at least, has an opportunity to add either a comment or a question.

- **Agreement for next steps.** The purpose of the presentation is to facilitate the client's decision. The worst outcome is no decision. You should manage the meeting in a way that allows for acceptable next steps if a final decision is not achievable at that time. The next steps to move the client towards a decision should be agreed, along with agreed timescales. Whatever the outcome of this stage, remember to thank the client for their time and the opportunity to work with them.

Rework the Elements that Missed the Mark

During or after the presentation, you may receive feedback or may have made your own judgement that there were elements that possibly missed the mark. Before a final decision is reached, you may have to rework a number of these elements before re-presenting.

At this point, you should expect that the amount of rework required is relatively minor. If it is not, you should consider re-qualifying the opportunity because this indicates a significant discrepancy between your understanding and that of the client. If you are prepared to continue, then the process iterates with amendment and re-presentation until the final decision is reached.

Once any necessary rework is completed, or if none was necessary, the outcome of this stage will be one of the following:

- **Green light – Proceed.** There are three options here:

  1. The client wishes to go forward, and you will deliver a further consulting piece, in which case you move forward to the Contracting step to re-enter at the Analyse step.

  2. The client wishes to go forward but your role is finished because some other party is taking the delivery forward. This may be a job well done or alternatively, a disappointment to you – if you were hoping to be involved in or to deliver the next phases.

  3. The client does wish to go forward, and you will deliver the proposed solution, in which case you move to the next Contracting step.

- **Amber light – Wait.** Consideration time or further client analysis is necessary. This amber light should be respected, and you should clearly understand the reasons for holding, any next actions that you are responsible for, any decisions that the client intends to make, and the timelines for any next steps.

- **Red light – Do not proceed.** The client does not wish to go forward with the recommendations and this particular journey finishes. This likely marks the end of the engagement. You may wish to investigate further as to why the solution is not acceptable, by requesting feedback. It also pays to collect and reflect on this decision, especially if a pattern can be discerned for the loss of the opportunity.

Contract for Delivery Engagement

Presentation may occasionally be the end of the engagement, but hopefully, in most cases, it is just the beginning. Assuming you have performed a thorough analysis, understood the client need, delivered a successful presentation, and agreed to continue with the engagement, you may be asked to deliver further work. If so, you will need to perform the Contracting step, outlined earlier, once again to document the next steps. This final Contracting step (the first two were performed after the Sales and Analyse steps respectively) may be the most important and high value so far for yourself and the client. The proposal itself could be large and complex compared to earlier analysis or recommendation activities, as it may cover part or all of an organisational change initiative. This complexity has a knock-on effect on pricing, contracting, and sign off.

When it comes to pricing a larger piece of work, there are a number of considerations. This may be an acceptable time to "discount to win", as you take advantage of a longer and larger commitment, or you may choose not to if you feel that value is already established. Whatever your strategy, it is likely that for larger pieces of work, the client will push for cost reduction because they, too, are looking to achieve the best possible outcome and not be locked into long-term commercially problematic agreements. You need to ensure that you are not pushed into something that is so low cost that it is difficult to deliver. Fair clients will recognise this, and it may be that extra value in terms of additional services are something to consider here, rather than cost reduction.

With the delivery engagement there will also likely be a more complex commercial agreement, including wider terms and conditions than at any previous phase, as with extra delivery complexity comes extra risk and, therefore, extra necessity to consider how to mitigate the risk. Your client may spend a longer time considering, specifying, and reviewing key terms and deliverables and you, personally, need to ensure you are spending sufficient time on governance to be certain that the agreement for work is viable and the terms solid.

And finally, you can expect that any sign off process will be more complex and last longer as clients and even your own organisation take more time to ensure that the agreement is acceptable from a commercial, risk, and delivery perspective. Commercial agreements tend to go higher up the organisation for review and approval as the amounts involved increase and the stakes get higher. This can prove problematic if you have to pipeline your work and find that delay affects this pipeline.

Contracting marks the end of the Advise stage and the beginning of the Act stage.

Key Practice 2 – Adding Value

At every stage, the consideration of what value both parties gain from the relationship should be considered because consultancy is fundamentally a value-based activity.

With rare exceptions, such as regulatory requirement, a client expects benefit in return for investment, usually a greater value than the initial outlay. So, as a consultant, you are constantly focusing on and considering value. You explain and reinforce the reasons why your services and solutions are valuable to the client. If you are unable to do so, then why would any client want to work with you or pay a price that you believe is fair?

The delivery of value for the money spent is of critical consideration to both parties throughout the consultant lifecycle. This section covers how the focus on value accumulates, considering it from both a quantitative and qualitative perspective. It also introduces two important techniques to visualise and communicate value: the return on investment analysis, and the project benefit map.

How Value Builds

Value builds throughout the consultant lifecycle and beyond, into each subsequent engagement. The ability to demonstrate value at one stage is valuable at a later stage. Adding value is therefore a cyclical activity where even at the end of a relationship with a client, the realised value can be used to demonstrate potential value to subsequent clients.

At all stages, the value proposition is more convincing if a hard currency amount can be attributed to it. This is quantitative benefit. Using forecasting techniques, you estimate the benefit in monetary units. You may want to specify optimistic, expected, and pessimistic financial values, since it is easy to overestimate potential benefit or to take credit for value which was realised for other reasons, or by other projects or synergies between initiatives.

The alternative to this is qualitative benefit. This includes things that are more difficult to measure in purely financial terms, such as increased quality or improved reputation. Qualitative benefits are also important because, if they wish, clients or potential customers can make their own extrapolations that translate into financial benefit.

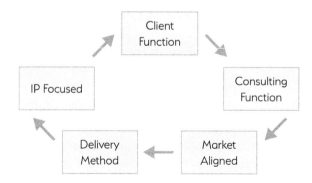

Figure 10. Value Cycle

The Five Stages of Value Building

Marketing: Examples of how engagements have led to value realisation.

Sales: Potential value from the specific engagement.

Analysis: Planned and expected value from the engagement.

Solutions delivery: Implementation of the deliverables with which value will be realised and managing to ensure value is retained.

Post-delivery: Measurement against the plan to ensure value is realised, captured, and used by client and consultant.

Marketing

Within marketing activities, as well as explaining the service or offering, you should refer to the benefit that could be realised if the client were to take up the service. This should be backed up by metrics you will have gathered during previous engagements and detailed in case studies of similar implementations. If this is an area in which you have not yet collected evidence, then referring to industry statistics or related numbers may help. Another way to gauge the realisation of value is to be explicit about your value proposition. Who gains benefit from your services and what is that benefit? You can phrase this simply as "I help x do y". This can form an important part of your "elevator pitch".

Sales

Early in the Sales step, previous successful examples of where value has been added should be quoted. At this point, every effort ought to be made to understand what the customer values. As talks progress to a more advanced stage, you will need to quantify how much value might be achieved for the customer and the relevance thereof to the customer's situation, which are steps necessary for any further progress to be made. Quantifying value and assessing its relevance are subsequently confirmed in the Analyse step.

Analysis

Within the Analysis phase, more precise figures are put on the expected benefit to correctly assess and recommend the effectiveness of the various options.

The assessment of both tangible quantitative benefit and less tangible qualitative benefit is a key part of the decision process. A financial analysis with a return on investment (ROI) graph is a core component of this step, as is the project benefit map (see later in the section), and it may be placed in a recommendations document or subsequent proposal. You or your client may also include the ROI graph in a business case document if part of the required steps include decision-making by an outside body.

Finally, as part of your proposal, you may want to measure the success of your delivery against the planned or expected benefit by creating KPIs or other business objectives on achieving hard numbers. You may also consider value-based pricing, which is where the cost of the solution is directly aligned to the value achieved. For example, the cost is 10% of the gross profit increase achieved by the client.

Solutions Delivery

Although benefits are primarily achieved after a solution is delivered, this period needs to maintain a constant focus on value in each of the constituent steps. This is done in the following four ways, to be discussed in detail in the section on Solutions Delivery (High-Performance Behaviours) in Chapter 4:

- First, by communication and reporting, where the progress towards achieving value is continually assessed and reported on.

- Second, by value control activities and change management, where any course corrections are implemented in such a way as to ensure that the value proposition of the project is not compromised.

- Third, by quick wins, which are interim or peripheral deliverables related to the project, and which provide immediate benefits.

THE CONSULTANT'S PLAYBOOK

- Fourth, by "value-add" activities. These are things that the client would perceive as valuable, that you can provide at little or no cost to the client, but typically are *not* related to the key engagement, but instead, are a benefit of working with you.

Post-Delivery

It is in the Post-Delivery phase that most value is realised, and the success of the project can finally be completely and accurately measured. Value is a cumulative phenomenon, and it may take a number of years to fully assess the change.

Measurements of cost against value should be regularly made and compared against the proposal and business case. It is best if this is done using the same factors as before to enable a direct comparison. This means that contact should be maintained between you and the client for considerable time after the official end of the engagement, though if this is not possible, you should provide the mechanisms for clients to track it themselves during offboarding.

Once collected, the information on achieved value can be used for a number of purposes:

- To justify the investment made by the client in the business case.
- To justify the investment made by the client in yourself.
- To provide confidence for the client that future initiatives will have a good chance of achieving a positive return.
- To provide you with further material that you can use for marketing opportunities, such as case studies or specific data.

If possible, you should collect this for other marketing and sales opportunities, thereby strengthening the value lifecycle.

Return on Investment Analysis

Value measurements can be quantitative, that is, assessed using numbers and often with specific focus on monetary units. One way in which to do this is a return on investment (ROI) analysis. This is a simple way of showing the effectiveness of an investment by comparing how much cost and how much return will be achieved at defined points over a period. This can be done either as a prediction for planned ROI, or as a way of measuring actual benefit against cost.

On an ROI Graph, both lines will have an upward trajectory, with spend typically rising first, and return, following. At some point the two lines cross and the point of ROI is achieved. The quicker the overlap, the quicker the ROI. If the lines never cross, then ROI will never be achieved, and any investment would be projected to lose money. The graph below indicates a typical ROI scenario where there is an upfront investment followed by continued regular costs, and the return starts later, but it eventually meets and overtakes the cost.

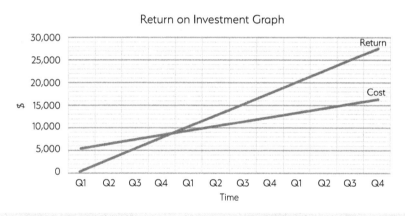

Components of an ROI Graph

Left hand axis: Monetary amount.

Bottom axis: Timescale.

Cost line. The cost of the project at projected points of the timescale.

Benefit line: The monetary benefit achieved at projected points of the timescale.

ROI is achieved at the crossing point of the two lines.

Figure 11. Return on Investment Graph

The quality of any ROI Graph is dependent on the quality of the data and the assumptions made. The relative trajectories of the lines and the length of time to cross indicate the level of risk in an investment.

Qualitative Benefit

Besides demonstrating benefit with financial values, you should also demonstrate qualitative benefit. Qualitative (or intangible) benefit is something which has value but is less easy to be measured financially. This can be further divided into measurable qualitative benefit and non-measurable qualitative benefit.

Measurable qualitative benefit is measured in ways that are not easily convertible to monetary values. Examples include:

- Increased employee satisfaction, measurable directly through engagement surveys, or indirectly through engagement indicators, such as attrition or unplanned absence.
- Increased client satisfaction, measurable through CSAT, NPS and CES scores (see the Glossary for a full definition).
- Increased quality, measurable through defect, issue, or incident metrics.
- Improved responsiveness, measurable through improved service level agreement (SLA) scores.
- Faster performance, measurable in a number of ways depending on the situation, such as speed-to-market.
- Greater capability, measured through capacity or skills metrics.
- Increased maturity, measured through industry-specific maturity indexes.
- Increased market share, measured through headcount and revenue metrics.

There are other qualitative benefits for which it may not be able to assign any kind of value at all. These include:

- Greater use of innovation, which has knock-on effects to employee engagement, and reputation.
- Higher buy-in to the project or change, and consequently, greater success in project outcomes.
- Improved communication, leading to higher engagement and smoother information flow.

- Improved client reputation and brand recognition, meaning the client is more attractive to potential employees, and to their industry as whole.

Although qualitative benefits may lead to quantitative benefit, the important factor is that they are worth achieving on their own merits and, therefore, highlighting to clients, especially if they match a client's particular issue or need.

Value-Add

As a consultant, you have a value proposition to deliver to the client, and it involves the concept of "adding value". But there is a very similar but distinct concept called "value-add" that exists in addition to "adding value". Value-add typically involves things that the client would perceive as valuable, though perhaps peripheral to the core solution you are providing. The ability to create value-add can provide a great differentiation between yourself and your competitors. A consultant who not only delivers what they agreed to but also delivers something additional (of value), will be viewed favourably by the client. Specific value-adds depend on your specific experience. Most value-add activities, however, fall into one of the following categories:

Education/Training

Providing formal or informal education through a variety of methods is a prime value-add. Using coaching, mentoring, or training sessions, or even providing important educational material, such as articles or other printed material, will help build trust.

Investment Services

It is your choice as to what you charge and how. An investment engagement (with no charge applied or at cost) might be something that you consider offering, though you should practise extreme care in defining and limiting any such activity, and ensure it is of value to both the consultant and the client. One example of this could be a rewards system where for every defined number of days of consultancy performed, a free day is earned to be used on strategic initiatives that the client might otherwise have difficulty getting funding for.

Access to Knowledge

A consultant can easily add value to clients by freely sharing the knowledge, both formal and informal, that they have gathered in their career. Useful articles or templates that have been collected can be offered, and ideas (if approached sensitively and not too many at a time) are usually well received, too.

Access to other Experts in your Company or your Network

An advantage of consultancy is that your networks provide other people who can be tapped into quite quickly. This type of help is at various degrees of separation, ranging from your local team members to the wider organisation. If you are part of a larger organisation, this is what clients expect when they engage with a consultancy, and it should be one of your operating principles. In addition, your network may include those who are specialist in areas other than your own, who may be able to add their own value to the client through a referral.

Quick Wins

Quick wins are a foundation to effective change. However, they also have a purpose all of their own. By identifying small or interim products and demonstrating early progress, the client gains confidence, and if done correctly, an interim product is something that can be used.

Access to IP and Innovations

Each engagement brings a chance to store and reuse methods, processes, and other information. In each subsequent engagement, you have the chance to use what you have collected to ensure the next engagement is better than the last. Using experience, products that you have created, or information that you have codified from previous assignments on your prime delivery, is one form of value-add. A second form is using it on areas which are parallel to your prime delivery.

Benefit Mapping

A Benefit Map describes various facets of the benefits of implementing a solution to help people understand "why" a project is being run, and it allows them to see what is in it for them. It is a visual representation of six interconnecting elements, which together show the benefit of the project or delivery and how they relate to one another. The elements are:

- **Output** – deliverable from the project or implementation, such as system or process created

- **Change** – change of way of working

- **Outcome** – the result of a change of way of working

- **Benefits** – improvements resulting from outcome and the reason why projects occur

- **Value** – metrics applied to the benefit

- **Corporate objective** – corporate measurements that come from the organisation plan

Here is an example Benefit Map:

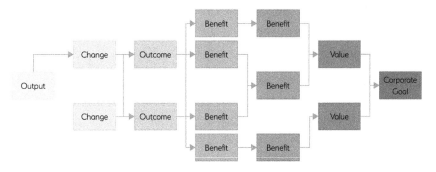

Figure 12. Benefit Map

THE CONSULTANT'S PLAYBOOK

A Benefit Map is an extremely useful tool as consultants always need to stress benefits and value. A Benefit Map:

• Provides a logical structure for describing value and how it is achieved.

• Provides clear definitions and differences between terms that are sometimes misunderstood.

• Shows the interactions of multiple factors and how value is achieved by the combinations of factors.

• Provides a visual alternative to dry lists of benefits and may resonate well with wider audiences.

• Allows for all types of measurable value and if necessary or helpful, can be further developed to describe the financial impact.

This is a technique that can be used at multiple points in your interactions with clients:

• During marketing, for example, by using case studies to demonstrate how previous clients have achieved benefit from engaging with you.

• During the Acquire stage when you are articulating the potential benefit of engaging with you.

• During the Advise stage when you are recommending why a certain option or solution is appropriate.

• When initiating the delivery, by using the potential benefit as the KPIs for measuring success.

• During the Solutions Delivery step and in particular in stakeholder management to stress the benefits to reluctant stakeholders and indicate what they will get from the delivery.

• And finally, for demonstrating value that has been added at the end of engagements.

One of the reasons this model is effective is that it provides a way of acknowledging the interactions between deliveries, and between projects, whether they are internal or external. In so doing, it helps in eliminating any double counting that may arise when multiple projects claim the benefit of change, when, in fact, they only have a part in developing it. A programme or organisational Benefit Map is therefore the natural extension.

4

ACT

Figure 13. The Consultant's Playbook Structure – Act Steps and Activities

Act is all about delivery. Not all engagements go further than the Advise stage, but for those that do, in order for them to be successful, it is recommended that well-managed initiation, delivery, and ending activities be executed. This chapter covers the process of taking the recommendations from the Advise stage and putting them into place through delivery.

Initiate

The objective of the Initiate step is to set up for successful delivery of the solution and to begin to nurture the relationship between yourself and the client.

By the end of the Advise stage and in conjunction with the client, you will have identified a solution that matches the client's true need and can now be implemented. Moving from solutions to delivery requires a change of pace.

Clients are looking for an early signal that the party they have brought in can deliver against what they need. The client is often watching closely in the early stages, and the first days set the mood for the rest of the engagement. For a consultant, a poor few first days can be difficult to recover from.

In addition, the client may well be under pressure from their senior management to demonstrate they have made a sound decision in bringing in an outsider. If the assignment is potentially of a longer term, they are also looking at the potential fit between you and the existing team. So you need to hit the ground running, quickly work out the culture, structure, and stakeholders, and if things do not go to plan, adapt.

The Initiate step includes three linked but distinct activities that set solid foundations and help you achieve this aim:

- **Consulting onboarding,** performing necessary activities that align you to the client's ways of working.

- **Client onboarding,** setting up your own systems and process to help you manage the engagement.

- **Delivery set-up,** setting up project mechanisms to help you manage your solutions delivery.

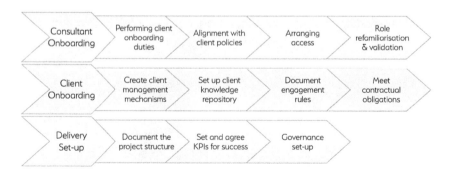

Figure 14. Initiate Process and Activities

128

Consultant Onboarding

When you first arrive at a client's site, you have a number of activities to perform that move you from a position as an outside party, to one who has at least the necessary characteristics of an internal party. That is, you transition to one who has all the required accesses and knowledge, and who has performed any necessary policy or other obligations. Where possible, you want to ensure that you and the client have done as much pre-work as possible so you can hit the ground running and minimum time is lost. Where activities cannot be performed in advance, they should be completed without delay. Consultant Onboarding should include the following activities:

Performing any Client Onboarding Duties

You may be expected to perform onboarding duties prior to, or immediately on arriving on-site. These will include completion of client onboarding processes, such as security awareness training, security checks, and site education. You may need to check other "day-one" expectations, such as who to meet, when, and where. You may also want to familiarise yourself with any locations, including transport or parking considerations, as well as mapping the local area for useful facilities.

Alignment with Client Policies and Protocols

In addition to general onboarding duties, there is a specific need to educate yourself on and align with client policies. As with any company, it is likely your client will have a number of policies that describe expectations for working for or with that organisation. These will be wide ranging and will likely include health and safety, diversity, security, wellbeing, complaints, and many others.

Arranging Accesses

A practical consideration is ensuring that you have the appropriate accesses to the resources you need to deliver your solution. This includes access to physical sites, IT systems, and information you may need for the engagement. It is worth noting that long onboarding processes have increasingly become the norm as financial and security due diligence requirements have steadily grown, and this may need to be factored into delivery timescales.

Role Refamiliarisation and Validation

The engagement may have developed or changed several times during the Sales and Contracting steps, and you will have derived further clarification on a number of things throughout the Initiate step. Some of this extra information will provide welcome clarity and certainty; however, at an extreme, it may cause you to question whether some or all of the elements of the solution that you proffered are still viable. At this point, it may become necessary to rework your proposal and contract, and you may need to reset expectations. Even if very little change has occurred, there could still be considerable elapsed time since the agreement was made. It is therefore important to refresh yourself on what is expected and when. It may be necessary to perform some personal knowledge transfer prior to starting the engagement by ensuring that any required pre-reading, information gathering, or other learning is done. This may include gathering templates, processes, and methods that you may need prior to engaging.

Client Onboarding

Client Onboarding is the process of setting up your own systems and performing any activities that are necessary when you engage or re-engage with a client. This stage is all about putting in place what is required for a long and successful relationship between yourself and the client. There are four activities to consider:

Create Client Management Mechanisms

Client management (or account management or client relationship management) is the overall set of methods and behaviours that are used to communicate with and service clients, and the corresponding methods used to enable business growth for the consultant or consultancy. At a very minimum, client management structures should include an engagement report, regular client meetings, and the setting up of your account plan for the client. More detail is contained in the "Managing the Client" section of the Solutions Delivery step, appearing later in the chapter.

Set Up Client Knowledge Repository

The client knowledge repository is where you store solutions and commercial or other delivery documents related to the engagement. The repository should include organisation of the material, methods that allow easy search functionality, and security. Kept in a repository, would be some or all of the following: contracts, deliverables, processes, templates, presentations, meeting minutes, notes, and communications. You are collecting all of your client interactions and knowledge, both formal and informal, so that you or another colleague can easily access information during or after the engagement, or potentially when re-engaging for the future.

Document Engagement Rules

The engagement rules make explicit how future commercial interactions should take place. To this point, both organisations have typically followed their own engagement processes, reacting to each other's ways of working, and learning about each other's specific needs. Once this initial engagement has started, it pays to document what has been learned so that future contractual interactions are clear, timely, and efficient. How requests are made, by whom and to who, what detail is included, and any authority levels (from your side and the client side) are all considered. In addition, how decisions are made and who needs to authorise along the way, should also be considered and documented for clarity. Finally, how invoicing and payment is dealt with. Whilst some of the latter is contractual, the actual logistics of getting payment is often surrounded by additional considerations, such as purchase orders and authorisation levels, so it may need further definition.

Meet Contractual Obligations

Depending on what you have agreed during the sales process, there may be specific contractual obligations to be implemented. These might include putting in place any of the specific measures, KPIs, or reports that you have agreed and are documented in the contract.

Delivery Set-Up

Whilst consultant onboarding and client onboarding are primarily about setting up the relationship, delivery set-up is the process of performing activities which are foundational in ensuring that you deliver on your commitments. Depending on the scale and scope of the delivery, you may need to perform some or all of the following:

Document the Project Structure

One of the first activities a consultant performs is structural. The process is the same whether you are part of a wider external team or are the sole consultant – you need to integrate yourself into the client environment whilst at the same time maintaining independence. To set up the structure, you need to create, publish, and agree where you fit into the client organisation, and how the reporting and communication structures will work between you and the client.

Set and Agree KPIs for Success

At the start of the engagement, you should define and agree the factors that are used to measure whether the solutions delivery is a success. These may even have been agreed within the contract as appropriate quality control measures. These factors are used continually throughout the delivery to maintain focus on what is important and are then also used to measure final success at the end of the engagement. The following six factors can be used as a basis for implementable KPIs:

- **Scope** – What are the deliverables and the content of the deliverables that you will create (the engagement parameters)?

- **Cost** – What is the expected cost for delivery?
- **Time** – What interim and overall timescales will you deliver by?
- **Quality** – How do you assess the quality of what has been delivered and what quality is acceptable?
- **Benefit** – What benefits and value will the client achieve through implementing the solution?
- **Satisfaction** – Is the client satisfied with the delivery and the engagement?

Governance Set-Up

Governance is the organisational set-up that helps direct and control the actions and affairs of management and others, ensuring that everyone does the right thing. For your purposes, governance ensures all parties are acting within the contracted agreement and are aligned with both client and consultant business objectives. If this is done diligently, it will improve the likelihood of meeting the objectives of the engagement. This part of the set-up phase includes agreeing the governance group and mechanisms, the standards and processes to ensure compliance, any authority levels for spend or decisions, the escalation routes, and any triggers for intervention.

Solutions Delivery

With the foundations you put in place during the Initiate step, you can move forward with confidence into the Solutions Delivery step.

The primary objective of the Solutions Delivery step is to deliver sustainable change through providing the agreed solution.

The actual content of your delivery is very much dependent on your expertise. For example, if you are an IT consultant, your delivery will focus on systems, applications, and technology. If you are a business process consultant, then it will focus on workflows, swim lanes, and process flows. It is out of the scope of this book to cover the subject matter that you are an expert in. Instead, this book focuses on common elements that occur across any type of successful delivery, which include:

- **High-performance delivery behaviours** – manifesting key behaviours to continually highlight effectiveness and value as a consultant.

- **Delivery management** – putting in place processes and systems to manage and deliver against the plan to ensure successful change across the whole organisation.

- **Dealing with problems** – managing and keeping away from common consultant hazards.

- **Client management** – setting up mechanisms to maximise the value of the relationship for both parties.

- **Building relationships** – proactive methods to increase closeness and trust on-site.

High-Performance Delivery

There are certain behaviours demonstrated and activities performed that contribute to a high performance and successful delivery, no matter what the subject matter of the delivery. High-performance behaviours are ways of acting that impart a positive message to the client. These are behaviours so integral to success that they become almost inseparable from any aspect of what is delivered to the client. High-performance activities on the other hand, are specific tasks or actions performed to enhance perceived and actual value for the client. These are discretionary in nature in that you need to choose when, where, and how to deploy them.

High-Performance Behaviours	High-Performance Activities
Delivery Focus	Quick Wins
Focus on Value	Using Leverage
Expertise and Differentiation	Communication
Consistency and Reliability	Being a Change Champion

High-Performance Behaviours

Delivery Focus

The most professional consultant, even one who communicates effectively, appears to have great customer insight, and works well in a team, will fail in their assignment if they do not deliver what is expected. There are some important exceptions and complexities, but fundamentally, this should be your highest priority.

What the client expects you to deliver can be encompassed by the three elements of the project triangle. If you deliver what you said you would (scope), when you said you would (time), to the budget agreed (cost) and all to an appropriate quality, then you have achieved your goal. The mantra of under-promise and over-deliver often generates some level of suspicion (what was wrong with the planning?) It pays to stick with the basics.

As well as being a fundamental goal on its own, successful delivery adds to your credibility and to your knowledge and learning, which means that you gain further opportunity with the client. It also allows you to publicise a successful engagement through case studies or references.

On the other hand, failure to deliver has a number of consequences. Besides causing potential reputational damage, contractual problems may also arise. Failure to deliver may prevent you from gaining further work with the existing client, and if you are forced to spend time and effort fixing the issue, there are potential opportunity costs because you cannot spend time with other clients on other engagements.

The question of whether you are delivering successfully, however, comes with a certain amount of complexity, certainly when larger scale or more complex deliveries are involved. Current views of success will change and what is considered an acceptable outcome may also change as risks and issues are managed, and plans adapted. Your delivery may have been based on certain assumptions, and even if your agreement is outcome-based, you will have caveats and triggers for known dependencies and things that are outside your control.

If one party has been overly political or demanding, or there were issues of wellbeing or mistreatment, for example, then even delivery can be trumped by more important value-based considerations. It is possible to do all the right things from your own perspective, have all the right elements in the contract, and yet still not come to an outcome that is acceptable to all. You will need to make up your own mind, depending on the specific circumstance. There may still be consequences, but at least you will feel good if you gave it everything and kept to your values.

In most circumstances, providing you and the client agreed what constitutes an acceptable delivery and you managed expectations well, even though this might not be what was originally planned or agreed, then this is perhaps the best measurement of delivery success.

Focus on Value

Consultancy is fundamentally a value-based activity. A client expects value in return for payment, usually a greater value than the initial outlay. So, as a consultant, you have to continually stress the value of your offering, that is, explain and reinforce the reasons why your services and solutions are valuable to the client. If you are unable to do so, then why would any client want to work with you or pay a price that you believe is fair? The delivery of value for the money spent is of critical consideration to both parties throughout the consultant lifecycle. You will find it useful to understand how the focus on value accumulates as well as considering it from both a quantitative (measurable) and qualitative (less easy to measure) perspective. Value is covered in depth in a later chapter.

The Solutions Delivery step is something of a no-man's land when it comes to value, with earlier steps very much about highlighting the value proposition (potential value) and later steps about realising the potential. Solutions Delivery is the point where, to a client, spend seems high and value realisation a distance away. You can mitigate this in a number of ways.

First, by **communication and reporting**, where the progress towards achieving value is continually assessed and reported on. Two key techniques that all consultants should be familiar with are **Return on**

Investment Analysis and **Benefit Mapping** (covered in Chapter 3 in the section on Adding Value). Both provide simple visual explanations of the value of the engagement and can be used continually as tools for maintaining a project-value focus.

Second, by **value control activities** and **change management**, where any course corrections are implemented in such a way as to ensure that the value proposition of the project is not compromised. This means explicit steps in key activities that analyse and highlight the value impact of all types of deliverable and engagement control.

Third, by **quick wins**, which are interim or peripheral deliverables, still related to the project, which provide immediate benefits. A good candidate for a quick win is easy to implement, has an outcome that is easy to see, and delivers a high impact for the effort.

And fourth, by **value-add** activities, as discussed earlier. As a consultant, you have a value proposition to deliver to the client through the main deliverables. But value-add is distinct. These are things the client would perceive as valuable, but which you can provide at little or no cost to the client. Typically, they are *not* related to the key engagement, but instead, are a benefit of working with you. These can include things such as education, access to your knowledge base or network, and access to any innovations.

Expertise and Differentiation

No matter how close the partnership with a client is, or how the relationship develops, you need to behave differently from the client's employees. Why is this?

Fundamentally, you are not a client employee. Even though you are on-site with client employees, you are an independent actor and placements at client sites are temporary. From their perspective, the client is not looking for another employee; rather, someone to solve a problem.

Secondly, clients often expect more from consultants than their own people, and once a relationship is established, as a consultant, you continue to differentiate yourself primarily through your expertise, knowledge, and the consequent quality of your work.

Finally, your value proposition relates to the quality of the services that are provided and some level of understanding that what you bring is unique or difficult to find. Perceived value is therefore closely related to expertise. Your credibility is related to your actions.

Your expertise and your capability are closely related. Ways in which to keep your expertise top of mind with a client, therefore, are the same ways in which you have developed and demonstrated your capability during earlier parts of the consultant lifecycle, but with the advantage that you have a specific audience identified and a relationship already built. These ways include providing education, content, and thought leadership materials in a measured way, always bearing in mind that you have to be careful not to take your own focus too far away from the delivery requirements.

Consistency and Reliability

Reliability is not just about delivering the outcome. Instead, it is more about the micro deliveries and ongoing behaviour as you progress towards the agreed goal. As a consultant, you are not only judged on the final delivery, but continually as you go about representing yourself through actions. Reliability is also a key factor in building trust.

Reliability is crucial because you are always under some level of scrutiny. Your reputation carries forward from one day to the next with clients, as well as from engagement to engagement. In addition, you are there to deliver something of importance to the client, which may well have dependencies on it. The appearance of reliability is therefore important in giving clients confidence that their larger plans are viable. Finally, clients pay a premium (and sometimes what they perceive to be a high daily rate) and expect to get what they pay for, especially if they had some level of mixed motivations in engaging with you in the first place.

One particular technique for maintaining reliability is called the **120/80/120 approach**, which is underpinned by the following factors:

First, it is difficult for any individual to operate consistently at 100% for a period of time; there are natural lulls in work and energy. Second, the client often remembers the beginning and the end of an engagement more clearly than the middle. The 120/80/120 approach recommends starting and ending with greater energy and drive, with the middle being more considered and with slightly reduced energy. The high energy start and end inject confidence in the client, with the start getting the foundations quickly in place and the end ensuring delivery. The middle period also has some tolerance and flex to enable the consultant time and energy to focus on urgent matters that arise.

High-Performance Activities

Quick Wins

Quick wins perform a useful role in embedding successful change. By identifying small or interim products and demonstrating early progress, the client gains confidence, and if done correctly, an interim product is something that can be used and that provides value. A good candidate for a quick win is easy to implement, with an outcome that is easy to see and has a high impact for the effort.

A client often expects an immediate return for their outlay. This is usually in excess of what they might expect a new permanent employee to provide. This does not mean that there is no time to learn, just that learning activities need to be approached with vigour and speed. It is best to intersperse learning in the first period with small deliveries or reports on progress. This gives the (accurate) impression that you are able to produce output quickly, that you can multitask, and that you are providing value immediately.

Using Leverage

Working with others as a consultant presents a unique challenge because you are expected to deliver results whilst rarely being in a position of organisational power. At best you have client management sponsorship, at worst, you have ineffective sponsorship and have to find other ways to get things done. You need to influence as you do not have actual authority.

The ability to "get things done" in any organisation, be it client or your own organisation, is rarely dependent on just title or position. In order to influence others, you need to understand your organisational leverage and increase your power. This takes time.

Certain things enable you to increase your leverage:

- **Results.** Reliably delivering great results for the company (consultancy and client).
- **Knowledge.** Having credibility through developing and demonstrating expertise.
- **Attitude.** Being the type of person who others like to work with by being helpful, approachable, and cooperative.
- **Empathy.** Understanding and appreciating the problems of others and being available for others to share their concerns.
- **Networks.** Building positive relationships and showing professional intimacy with others throughout client and consultancy organisations.
- **Inclusion.** Involving others in your decisions, activities, and project.
- **Detachment.** Having a degree of emotional detachment, allowing you to view things objectively and fairly, which can increase your standing.

Communication

Good delivery-communication has several characteristics that cover delivery, client, and relationship considerations. Ensuring your communication channels have these, will stand you in good stead. Your communications should strive for the following objectives:

- **Inclusive.** When considering delivery communication, you should spend time determining who to communicate with, and how you will deal with differing types of preferred communication requests due to varied communication styles. As a final consideration, your consultancy colleagues or management may also have requests that have to be included.

- **Varied delivery methods.** Good communication tends to cover multiple presentation types, including verbal, written, and visual. Online and remote deliveries need to be factored in where co-location is not possible.

- **Controlled.** Thought needs to be given to how communication requests can be managed and controlled. This includes formal ("I would like another report for this") and ad hoc ("Can you give me an update on ...?"). A certain amount of flexibility will be necessary, but continual requests for reports risk distracting from the core delivery.

- **Efficient.** Formal and informal communications can be onerous if they are not controlled, and even if they are, may still be quite demanding. It is important that you find efficient ways of collating or providing information so that communication is easy to deliver and manage.

- **High quality.** In order to be trusted, communications must have a variety of quality characteristics, such as being informative, understandable, relevant, accurate, and honest.

Being a Change Champion

Consultants are in a position of influence, typically not power, so championing is one of the tools to ensure successful organisational change on behalf of their client.

There are a number of options to help ensure that the delivery is successful, and that change has the greatest chance of embedding:

- **Champion, Communicate, Campaign.** Continually educate on the scope, benefits, and reason for the change. Show people how the changes work and how this affects them. Continual education of the value of the change helps reduce people's fear.

- **Accept help.** Change will fail without people believing in or agreeing with the need for change. Buy-in needs high level and on-the-ground support. Through listening to, questioning, and accepting help from people across the organisation, a broad consensus can be achieved because people feel empowered and involved.

- **Advocate.** This involves creation and communication of the vision, along with the reasons for it. Without a vision, there is no reason for anything to change.

- **Noteworthy wins.** Quick wins or small wins are noteworthy in that they give people reason to celebrate, and they provide confidence that the change journey ahead will provide the expected results. This in turn increases morale and builds support on the way to the overall vision.

- **Govern.** Find methods to monitor uptake and to ensure that the changes are applied across the organisation, concentrating on those key groups that have the potential to make or break success.

- **Energy.** It is easy to lose momentum after the early successes and when the excitement of novelty has gone. Momentum requires hard work and consistency as well as personal investment.

Delivery Management

Project or delivery management is a topic fully deserving of its own book. Therefore, what is included here is a simplified description of five key delivery management activities for consultants.

The five key areas are:

- Planning
- Change control
- Risk and issue management
- Reporting
- Stakeholder management

Planning

Figure 15. Planning Process

A plan of one type or another is the backbone of any delivery. Planning answers the questions: what tasks are being delivered, by whom, and when is each task being delivered? The questions provide actions and goals to be reported against and then controlled.

A simple planning process that a consultant might use for a sequential process would go as follows:

1 **Develop a task list.** Brainstorm or use previous experience to produce a work breakdown structure to document the tasks required for each deliverable.

2 **Add dependencies.** Organise the tasks so those that can only be started or completed after others are ordered correctly and explicitly linked.

3 **Estimate.** Provide top-down estimates for major deliverables and bottom-up estimates for each task. Compare and adjust so that they align.

4 **Allocate the task.** Find and assign a responsible party for the completion of each task.

5 **Create a schedule.** For each task, plan a start and completion date, taking into account dependencies, expected effort, and availability of resources.

6 **Monitor and report.** Progress reports set out the deliverables and objectives of the project and the purpose of comparing the actual position, usually related to finance, effort, time, and value realisation. Reports are usually sent out at regular intervals and need to be succinct, clear, and accurate.

7 **Adjust where necessary.** To control the delivery, adjust the plan when the plan is no longer valid.

There are times when, through your own making or for other reasons, you are not able to deliver all you said you would. The most important thing is to communicate at the right time (usually the earlier, the better) that this cannot be achieved. A consultant is expected to be proactive at this point and should offer a variety of options along with a recommendation.

Any sign that the consultant is throwing the problem back to the client is bound to frustrate.

Change Control

Figure 16. Change Control Process

Consultancy requires a significant amount of adaptability as engagement priorities can change frequently. Significant change of scope, timescales, or priorities means that contractual and planning agreements have to be re-assessed. What is to be delivered, when, and to what quality may need to be re-baselined. This is called "change control" or "change management". Poor change management can ruin a delivery, causing scope, cost, or timescales objectives to miss being met. The initial response to a change of parameters should be to consider how this change can be supported, and done so in a controlled, managed manner.

Small changes may be incorporated with minimum deviation. In this case, a reconfirming email detailing the new agreement, sent from the consultant or account manager to the client, is all that is needed.

Larger changes will probably require negotiation on other elements that need to be deprioritised. Sometimes an engagement cannot be easily changed.

Significant contract deviation will need contract renegotiation to an extent that may not be tolerable or practical. And you or your consultancy may not have the skills to deliver to the new, changed requirements.

Change control is, therefore, an important process for projects and for engagements. A change control process should be created and followed for change to be managed effectively. This process should be capable of covering project change and contractual change.

The change control process involves the following sequential activities:

1 **Request.** This can come from both directions, either the client or the consultant.

2 **Impact analysis.** The change is analysed for its impact on cost, effort, timeliness, dependencies, and consequences, especially the impact on value realisation.

3 **Decide.** A change committee (at the very least including a client member and the consultant) makes a decision based on the impact. The outcome will be one of the following:

   a. Approved

   b. Partly approved

   c. More information necessary

   d. Escalation needed

   e. Not approved

4 **Deliver.** The agreed change is delivered and all documentation, including plans, specifications, and contracts are updated to reflect the new understanding.

Risk and Issue Management Processes

Figure 17. Risk and Issue Management Process

Risks are issues that may or may not occur, and issues are risks that have become reality. Because both are related, the techniques and systems to deal with each are similar.

Depending on the size and importance of the engagement and the client, you might find it beneficial to set up a risk management process and log any client-specific risks that you might note. These will not only relate to the delivery itself but will also cover the service and client management aspects.

A simple risk management process for a consultant is as follows:

1 **Identify risk.** Risks can be identified through proactive means, such as workshops, or may be identified as they are found. Risks should be centrally captured in a risk log, and fully and accurately described. Any party should be able to identify a risk, which helps gather a comprehensive set of risks for all project areas or functions.

2 **Analyse.** Further analysis is then performed, primarily to understand the likelihood and impact of the risk occurring. These are typically scored on a scale of 1 to 5, and the risk score is calculated by multiplying the two scores together. Higher risks receive a higher score. Risks should also be categorised by type.

3 **Manage and monitor.** After analysis, risks are allocated to a party to manage and decisions are made on how to manage the risk, whether to avoid the risk completely, mitigate the risk, or accept the risk. The status of risk continues to be monitored as actions are put in place, and occasional risk audits can be introduced to further strengthen the process.

4 **Report.** As part of overall management, risk reports that are accurate and complete should be regularly produced and appropriately circulated to the correct audience.

Although the process above refers to risks, it is possible to follow exactly the same steps when managing issues. The risk log identified in the first step can therefore be both a risk and an issue log. The following table describes the data that you would capture for both and store in the log:

Field	Description
Risk/Issue Reference	A unique identifier.
Title	A brief summary title to help reference.
Type	Risk or issue?
Date Raised	When the item was entered into the log.
Raised By	Who identified the item?
Category	The category of the risk or issue – dependent on your systems and functions.
Likelihood	For risk only. Typically scored on a scale of 1 to 5, with 5 being the highest likelihood of occurrence.

Field	Description
Impact	The risk and issue impact, based on a scale of 1 to 5, with 5 indicating the highest impact.
Risk Rating	For risk only. The multiplication of likelihood and impact, with a higher number being the higher risk.
Description	Detailed description of the risk or issue – sufficient to enable impact analysis.
Decision	Whether to accept, avoid, or mitigate the risk or issue.
Update	Further updates as the risk or issue is monitored.
Status	Current status – Is the risk or issue live?
Owner	Who is responsible for managing the risk or issue?

Reporting

The purpose of reporting is to communicate project or delivery progress to your stakeholders. It fulfils the dual purpose of informing stakeholders about project health and injecting confidence in the project by careful and accurate communication. It is worth noting that the reporting we are talking about here is regular project delivery reporting, not project summary reporting or client engagement reporting, which have separate purposes. Regular reporting, when performed well, reduces overall project work by streamlining what you require and what you need to do to communicate with interested parties, and by removing necessary status meetings.

A first consideration for any reporting is the audience. Your audience is, broadly speaking, your full group of stakeholders, though not all stakeholders will receive the same report. In fact, as a principle, the level and detail of reporting should vary by audience. Too little detail, or the wrong focus for a given person or group, will not serve the general purpose of transmitting useful information. On the other hand, too much information may overwhelm and result in important information for that group being hidden or passed over. Some information may not be appropriate, for example, commercial or confidential data, so it is worth considering several versions of a report – if this can be done without too much inefficiency.

Effective reporting has a number of characteristics based on good communication principles. These are:

- **Regular**, but only so much as to be helpful – daily, weekly, monthly reports are all appropriate for different purposes.
- **Timed** to be purposeful so that it can be read and actioned without delay, or without being missed because of other communications or reports.
- **Appropriately pitched** so that senior parties can intervene and control without encroaching on the responsibilities of other parties.
- **Concise**, and while it is not a hard and fast rule, something that can fit on a single page, or perhaps two, may be sufficient for a more regular report.
- **Clear** so that key messages are obvious and unambiguous.
- **Efficient.** If it can be automated with tools such as business intelligence software, then all the better.
- **Attractive.** It uses visuals where helpful or other methods to attract the reader to key messages or to the report as a whole.

Finally, you should consider the structure and contents of the report. A progress report is fundamentally a combination of three types of information: summary information, analysis, and data, which, together, contain progress of the delivery against the plan. The table below provides an adequate structure:

Section	Description
Unique ID	A report should be named for clarity and dated for uniqueness.
Project Status	Typically, a RAG (Red, Amber, Green) status or sometimes a more descriptive piece of text.
Management Summary	A paragraph containing several key pieces of information related to the project status.
Area/Function Detail	Each function, area, task, or milestone that is in progress should be included at a minimum. You may also include not-yet-started or completed tasks. Finally, you may consider including specific contractual areas covering KPIs and key deliverables. For each element, you should cover progress against plan, as well as projections and upcoming targets. Any blockers should be highlighted.

Section	Description
Risks and Issues	Risks and issues might be included, especially high risks or live issues, or a link to the log included.
Financials	Actual versus budgeted expenditure to this period and projections for the future.
Value Analysis	Any value that has been realised by the project so far should be qualified and quantified. When combined with the financial report from the section above, this can provide a return on investment analysis.
Important Links	Links to other useful management elements, such as the business case, change log, or risk log to enable easy access for project stakeholders.

Stakeholder Management

Figure 18. Stakeholder Management Process

Stakeholder management is the process of identifying and managing people who are affected in some way by the project you are delivering, and then putting in place activities that ensure these stakeholders act so as to help rather than hinder the successful implementation.

Stakeholder Identification

Stakeholders are people who pay for the project, provide resources, stand to benefit from the project in any way, or have some other form of vested interest in the outcome. They can be internal to the project or external. In addition, anyone who is impacted by the project may be a stakeholder, though you may more accurately think of these as secondary stakeholders and those with more direct impact as primary stakeholders. Once identified, you should record these in a stakeholder log.

Stakeholder Mapping

Once identified, you can begin the process of stakeholder mapping, which helps you in understanding the role and importance of stakeholders *before* you start the process of managing them. There are a number of ways in which you can map. Here is an example of a matrix that categorises stakeholders according to their power over your work, and their interest in it, and places these two variables on the two axes of a Power/Interest Grid. Where you place a stakeholder on the grid, indicates how you will need to manage them during the engagement.

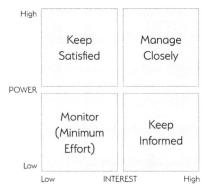

Components of a Stakeholder Grid

High power, high interest (Manage Closely): Fully engage these people, work hard to communicate, and satisfy them.

High power, low interest (Keep Satisfied): Put sufficient effort in with these people to keep them content.

Low power, high interested (Keep Informed): Adequately communicate to ensure no major issues arise and use them to provide help for you.

Low power, low interest (Monitor): Monitor them and provide occasional communication.

Figure 19. Stakeholder Grid

Stakeholder Meeting

Once you have mapped your stakeholders, you should develop a plan to manage them. This begins with meeting them and understanding what matters to them, and whether they support your project. Start to build relationships and trust amongst them. At this point, you will also be able to form a view whether they are in the right position on the grid, and whether you need to work to move them to a different viewpoint.

Stakeholder Strategy

The data collected from the meeting and its analysis, allows you to develop your strategy for managing the individuals. Individual or group strategies should be created for each stakeholder or stakeholder group to allow you to develop maximum value (which may include removing them as a blockage) and move them into your desired state. For stakeholders who may need to move into a more positive position, you should state what is in it for them, involve them in planning, meet regularly with them, and take their input. Communications plays a large role in stakeholder management, and you should have both overall and individual stakeholder communication plans in order to keep them informed. For each individual, you should consider the regularity of communications and the content.

Dealing with Problems

As well as demonstrating positive attitudes and attributes, a consultant will need to react to difficult situations that arise. These are to be expected! How a consultant reacts can have wide impacts. A certain amount of resilience is necessary in these situations, as is an understanding that most situations can be resolved with honest communication and good intentions.

If the client does not want you there. This is a surprisingly familiar situation and manifests in various forms. It often occurs because of the mixture of need and fear that many clients exhibit. A consultant should establish exactly what behaviour is giving rise to the issue and its source. If it can be established that a) the client who feels this way is the key stakeholder in the consultant–client relationship, and that b) the client has a particularly pressing concern or fear, then a consultant may attempt to address this particular fear. If this concern is more fundamental and the key client really has significant misgivings about why you are there, then this needs to be addressed in a head-on manner with them.

If you are working with ineffective client employees. Honest but helpful appraisal is a necessary skill that consultants need to practise in their many dealings with client employees. It is not always necessary to give feedback on any individual, but it may become so if you are asked to provide it, or if the employee is affecting your work. Three principles are important: First, you need to collect evidence and examples for your input to be effective. Second, any feedback given should be constructive and honest. Third, it is important not to generalise. *Never* indicate that you believe that consultancy employees are intrinsically more capable than client employees.

If the client already knows the answer. A common frustration for permanent client employees exists when senior management engage consultants to say or do something that permanent employees have been saying or doing all along, but their work or views have not been recognised. In this situation, it is ethical to acknowledge this and wise to attempt to consult with those employees. A difficult situation might be transformed into a win through transparency.

If you cannot get enough internal support. The onus is on the consultant to ensure that they are doing everything possible to help the client. This may mean bridging the gap if a client is not always upholding their end of the bargain. This is the price that consultants pay for helping clients, who often hire them to mitigate their own shortcomings. However, there are limits to how much extra a consultant can take on. If the lack of support is preventing sufficient progress towards agreed objectives, then this must be raised with the client.

If the assignment does not play to your strengths. Consultants who can flex up, down, and sideways are immensely valued by clients. Though, consultants, like all people, have their own career objectives and day-to-day preferences on what work suits them, and while it is possible to adapt temporarily to ill-fitting roles, in the long term this is unlikely to be sustainable. If you have stated your needs upfront during the Advise stage, refer back to this agreement and attempt to come to a medium-term agreement that meets these needs.

If you have been engaged to perform activities under poor conditions. Sometimes consultants are engaged to do work under conditions that would potentially burn out or disengage permanent employees. In fact, this may be the specific reason why outside help has been sought. If you are an external or independent consultant, whether you accept this work (or continue in it if you have already started) is entirely up to you. It may be something that you can cope with for short periods, though continual stresses will, of course, affect your wellbeing. If the client is pressuring you to continue, or has been disingenuous about conditions, an assertive response explaining the situation is necessary. This should go through an escalation process until the situation is resolved or you exit from the assignment.

Self-Inflicted Wounds

In addition, there are a number of problems that consultants can inflict on themselves. This requires an awareness and an ability to recognise their presence, as well as the strength not to follow the temptations that they sometimes provide.

- **Overstepping professional boundaries.** At times, a consultant can unintentionally misunderstand the nature of the personal/professional relationship. Much of the basis of successful consultancy and teamwork comes from working hard to develop amicable relationships. You can easily forget that other people do the same thing. As such, the working relationship is partly artificial. This artifice sometimes causes us to forget the real reason for our presence is to solve a client problem. Some of our natural behaviours can cause problems on the client site and can affect the consultant–client relationship.

- **Going native.** Occasionally, a consultant starts to identify with the client more than with the consultancy. It often happens if the consultant is on-site for a long time, or (for those consultants who are part of a larger consultancy) if contact with colleagues and the consultancy is limited. A consultant needs to be aware if they see signs that either they, or consultants they are with, have begun to exhibit signs of this.

- **Playing politics.** Internal organisational politics are hard to avoid, yet for long-term security of assignments, a consultant must navigate these waters effectively. Politics can manifest in a number of overt and subtle ways but is always characterised by an individual or group's desire to promote a point of view at the expense of others. The consultant needs to recognise political behaviour, navigate around it where they can, and strive not to be part of it. It is not always possible to avoid the impact of politics or political behaviour, but "playing politics" does not reflect well.

- **Gossip.** People who gossip can be perceived as unreliable, time wasters, and malicious. An assumption is that if a person exhibits such behaviour, that reflects how they act on a more regular basis. This is the antithesis of how it is expected a consultant should behave and such behaviour should be avoided.

- **Over-promising.** Professing competence in an area that you are only fleetingly familiar with, or emphasising your credentials based on experience that was limited at best, are both examples of over-promising. This type of behaviour will likely result in you being found out and its consequence is broken trust. Short-term financial gain is rarely worth it when compared to under-delivering to your client or having a damaged reputation. Instead, be honest with your appraisal and experience and set the right expectations; it is far better in the long term.

- **Using client time to upskill.** While you aren't supposed to know everything about your client when you commence, you are certainly supposed to have control of your craft. If you do not, it is up to you to fix this in your own time. The client is paying a fee for expertise and results and is expecting a fully formed response to their needs. This includes you, the consultant. There may be occasions where both parties agree to go forward into an engagement where this is not the case, but this must be explicitly understood and covered in the Acquire stage.

- **Having a different agenda.** From any engagement, you will have your own goals and objectives that are not the clients, such as the desire to gain additional domain or functional experience, or to create a case study. However, if your agenda conflicts with your client's, or there is potential conflict of interest, it will cause frustration with the client, and possible engagement failure when they come to realise this.

- **Maintaining too much distance.** "Going native" can cause problems for the consultant but so, too, can maintaining too great a distance between yourself and the client. Relationship establishment requires proximity and a certain amount of getting to know the real you. If you are "all business" and don't take social opportunities, it may be hard for you to build trust in the client's eyes.

- **Talking a different "language".** Most organisations use their own terms and language for the work they do, the roles they perform, or what they produce. You, on the other hand, have probably worked towards using a consistent terminology for your services and processes. There will always be a greater or lesser difference between the two language sets. Insisting on your own terminology in contracts, services, deliverables, or other communications, may well lead to a lack of understanding. It is usually up to you to adapt to the client's preferred terms unless terminology is part of the problem or a sign of something more serious underneath.

Client Management

Client Management is the activity of engaging with the client to maximise the value of the relationship for both parties. (Value is a key topic discussed in chapter 3.) In order to do this, you have to set up touchpoints which are over and above any others that cover the solutions delivery. The touchpoints need to be regular and structured to achieve the required outcomes and, like most things in the consultant–client relationship, the onus is typically on things being consultant driven rather than client driven. The two major touchpoints to help manage the client are through meetings and reports. In addition, account planning is a key technique used to control and plan your interactions with any individual client and in so doing, help you achieve the value you hope for from each client.

Account Meetings

The account meeting provides the best opportunity for regular contact, which is necessary to build relationships and to receive client input on future requirements and client satisfaction. Topics for discussion in the meeting include a reminder of current engagements, a summary of the value provided, upcoming client change pipeline, and any potential services not currently provided that may be relevant to the client's situation. Not all clients believe in the need for account meetings, seeing it as a half-hidden attempt to sell more services. Whilst it is important to respect client opinion on the amount of contact required, if there is a significant gap between client and consultancy expectations, then it is likely that the balance will swing naturally to how much the client wishes to meet, and this may not be healthy for the relationship in the long run.

Regular Engagement Report

A consultant engagement report describes and summarises the totality of the engagement between client and consultant. It is aimed at the strategic and governance level, rather than a detailed project or tactical level, unlike the project or delivery report. It is a key document for consultants to describe to the client the value and benefits of engaging, and it is a key document for clients who want to check the value of, and justify the investment in, the consultant. The report should be produced at regular intervals – such as monthly, three-monthly, or perhaps six-monthly. It should include key discussions held, delivery updates, costs of engagement, benefits realised, and any value-adds to the provided service.

Account Plan

The purpose of an account plan is to document key information about the client to aid with planning and to be referred to when needed. Included in the plan may be client budgets, media releases and company information, contact information, upcoming projects, and any identified pipeline of potential work. When completing the plan, you should map and show the client organisation, identifying individuals you have relationships with, identifying which individuals you should have relationships with, and at what levels you have penetration. Not all accounts need account plans; the greatest return on investment from this kind of activity comes from larger accounts.

Contract Monitoring

Continued awareness of the contractual situation with regard to the engagement is necessary. It is all too easy to run out of allocated time either by "burning up" the agreed effort, or by approaching the end date of an agreement without having either completed all necessary deliverables or having negotiated an extension or renewal to an ongoing assignment. Effective account management requires that you are proactive regarding commercial matters so there is clarity for both parties and the risk of working without appropriate contractual coverage is minimised.

Building Relationships

Building relationships is critical to the short- and long-term success of consultants. Key relationships must be nurtured. Your ability to quickly build rapport with clients on-site, which can move over time to long-lasting relationships, is one of the most important building blocks of success.

Good relationships lead to better collaboration, more tolerance when things go wrong, and ultimately a greater likelihood of achieving project goals. It also makes it easier for someone to pick up the phone when your services might be required again in the future. A history of friendly interaction helps buffer against occasional stresses and tense situations.

A consultant has a need to maintain and grow their own business as well as deliver on behalf of another party. The relationships developed when engaging with one client, often recur at subsequent points in a consultant's career. It is a truth of the consulting business that people like to work with people whom they have worked with before. The stronger the relationships that are built over time, the more likely that you will be remembered when a team is being assembled in the future.

THE CONSULTANT'S PLAYBOOK

Building relationships is not just simply talking to people; it is finding time to take a real interest in them, their viewpoints, and how you interact with them. In the initial stages of a relationship, this requires effort until a more comfortable point is reached. In some cases, a work relationship will reach a stage where both parties do not really consider it an effort to maintain. However, it usually takes years to achieve this stage. In the meantime, go out of your way to say "hello", ask meaningful questions, and take an interest in both the person and their work.

There can be counterproductive relationships, of course. Watch out for clustering (spending time with similar people) and layering (spending time with people of the same level), both of which limit your world view.

Building relationships is an individual activity that benefits more than just the job at hand. In whichever way your connections are built, they prove useful at almost every point in your career and at every activity.

Building On-Site Relationships

When starting on a new project, you are often beginning from scratch with your relationships. This early period is critical to making the later engagements work. Without distracting from your delivery focus, time needs to be spent mapping the team, and introducing yourself. Teamwork is one of the most important factors determining project success.

It is important to develop wider relationships in the organisations that you are assigned to. There is always opportunity to solve other problems for the organisation, and other potential sponsors or supporters can develop or be acquired if they can see the benefit of working with you. There are three key principles to effective on-site relationship building:

- **Be easy to work with.** Be helpful at work when people ask and be proactive with help when you see an opportunity. As a consultant, being helpful to your direct client is expected. It is the extended team where this pays dividends in getting to know others and encouraging reciprocal behaviour. Be easy to approach and you will find that people approach you.

- **Seek out opportunities for interaction.** Introduce yourself to your immediate client team members as you encounter them. Then identify the people you need to know outside of this group who will help you achieve your goals. Make an appointment, talk about something you have in common, or go to them with some thoughts and ideas about what might help them. Make social media connections with people you meet and with those you want to meet.

- **Take up opportunities to meet people.** Grab chances when they present themselves, such as greeting people at coffee machines and dining areas, asking someone after the meeting how it went, attending client functions or after-work events, or introducing yourself to attendees at meetings if you have not met them before.

Six Rules to Build Relationships

In the list below are six simple but important ways of behaving, which, if you follow them, can help you build long-lasting and wider-ranging relationships. They are divided into two categories: those actions that make people feel comfortable (and therefore happy to spend time with you), and those that make them feel important (and therefore you cater to their basic needs).

Whilst the ideas are simple, you need to make an effort, take time, and often step out of your comfort zone to make them effective.

Make Others Comfortable

1 **Spend time with people.** Relationships take time to build. You need to devote time to others. The more you devote, the easier it becomes to devote even further time. It also means that when you cannot devote time, sufficient groundwork has been laid for this not to cause the relationship to stutter or become uncomfortable.

2 **Use the other person's preferred communication style.** Speak in a way that is comfortable for others by identifying their communication style and adapting to it. There are a number of frameworks you can use, but whichever one you choose, it is you who, as a consultant, has to make the adaptation.

3 **Show vulnerability.** Building relationships is a matter of slowly getting to know another person. One way in which to accelerate this can be to show some vulnerability and thereby demonstrate that you are prepared to trust that person with sensitive information.

Make Others Feel Important

1 **Show interest in others.** By giving people attention, asking them questions, and remaining focused on them, you communicate to them that you respect them, their time, and their values. People who are shown this kind of attention have an emotional reaction and are drawn to seek this out in the future.

2 **Give them the right kind of appreciation.** People feel valued when appreciation is given in a language that they understand. Some people prefer words of appreciation, others having someone spend time with them, others enjoy acts of service, and others again, physical or tangible gifts. Conversely, the wrong type of appreciation can mean little.

3 **Remember them.** There is little more soul destroying that not being remembered by someone who you remember. And as a consultant, this may be your one and only chance to commence a relationship. So try to remember names and a little bit about someone and show them they are important enough to stay in your mind (and hopefully they really are!).

End

It is the combination of knowledge and experience, in conjunction with the identified core skills and consultancy activities, which roll up into the activity of client or project delivery. Everything works towards this and without a successful delivery, a professional consultant has not performed. Although, even if the delivery is exceptional, it is possible to fail at the very last hurdle if the engagement is not completed thoroughly and professionally.

The objective of the End step is to ensure that the solution has been delivered, that the benefits are capable of being realised, and the relationship is strengthened.

It is an interesting quirk of human memory that it is the beginning and the end of events that stick in the mind the most, which means that the finish of an assignment can have a considerable impact on the success of the engagement compared to the length of the activity. You need to ensure that you finish at full speed, rather than drifting out of the engagement. This also allows you to wrap up with time to spare, allowing capacity for unforeseen final events.

A good ending is planned; it should never be a surprise that the engagement has finished. What you do at the end should be considered at the beginning. The activities in the End step, therefore, mirror the activities in the Initiate steps and include one final activity to ensure that work continues. The four activities are:

- **Delivery breakdown** to ensure products are delivered and value is realised.

- **Consultant offboarding** to collect and summarise your own information for future use.

- **Client offboarding** to leave the client with the best possible experience and a clear end to the engagement.

- **Moving to the next engagement** either with the current client or elsewhere.

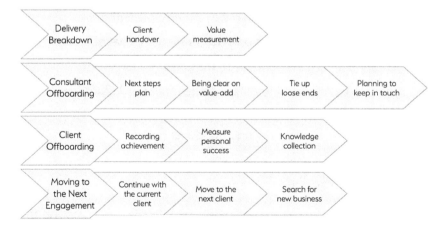

Figure 20. End Process and Activities

Delivery Breakdown

Your priority is to ensure that you deliver what you said you would deliver. Of course, validation of this should have been going on throughout the engagement, but the End steps must include a formal handover and measurement of success. Doing this properly means that there is a clean and clear end to the assignment, which increases the chance of successful realisation of benefits after you have left and stays in the client's mind as a successful engagement of a consultant. Client handover and value measurement, therefore, are the two key components of a successful delivery breakdown.

Client Handover

Whatever the delivery, the client will eventually take charge. Consequently, there is a process of moving control of any items from the project to the client. This is sometimes referred to moving to a "business as usual" approach. This activity performs the dual purpose of ending consultant control and delivering the solution to the client for their ongoing use. Without a formal handover, you risk making a strong engagement a perceived failure by falling at the final hurdle. The following steps are necessary to perform a handover properly, and their associated activities include:

- Identifying the handover audience and sign off authority.
- Comparing the deliverables produced with the deliverables specified.
- Documenting and sending this to the client.
- Creating educational material to ensure that knowledge is not lost to the client when you leave.
- Presenting the educational and handover material.
- Performing any knowledge transfer.
- Asking for (and achieving!) sign off.

Finally, as part of the client handover, a high-level report detailing the delivery should be produced. Did you deliver what you said you would, to the costs agreed, when you said you would, and to the agreed quality?

With the client's involvement, measure yourself against the success criteria you created in the Initiate step.

Value Measurement

Once the handover is in progress or has been completed, you have to address the value of the delivery, which is a vital component of the assessment to determine whether the engagement has been a success. For consultants, there are five ways in which you can consider success:

1 **Delivery.** Did you deliver everything you said that you would? Your contract may state the products or outcomes, but you may also have other deliverables that you have committed to during the engagement.

2 **Personal performance.** Did you match the values and the culture of the client, and did you perform to the best of your abilities? Feedback from your client should be sought and listened to.

3 **Impact on the client.** Did your intervention result in meaningful change that will be effective in the longer term, not just when you are present?

4 **Business growth.** Did the assignment have a positive effect on your business? Did your reputation or capability increase? Did you procure further business, either within the existing client or elsewhere?

5 **Benefit.** Did the implemented solution deliver the benefits you stated it would? This assessment should be done by comparing the benefit seen against the potential benefit you proffered in the Solutions Delivery step, though this may not be possible to consider yet since it depends on where you are in the lifecycle of the change.

Consultant Offboarding

Client Offboarding is the process of moving yourself out of the client environment. During this process, the client management aspects of the engagement are completed and both parties move to a post-engagement mindset so that the client no longer has specific things they are expecting from you.

Create a Next Steps Plan

A consultant should aim to ensure that any deliveries are sustainable and that there is a realistic plan to use them. If relevant or necessary, a "next steps" plan should be provided to help maximise the chances that the deliveries are embedding within the organisation.

A next steps plan can be as simple as a list of actions for the client, or a more complex deliverable, such as a Gantt chart or document, with tasks, dates, and responsibilities specified. What is included in the next steps plan should be a logical progression from what has come immediately before. For example:

- If you delivered a review, the next steps might be a set of recommendations.

- If you delivered a set of recommendations, the next step might be a plan for change.

- If you delivered a plan for change, then the next step might be the implementation of the change.

- If you delivered the change, the next steps might be tracking the benefit realisation.

The next steps plan may involve you, but even if you are not involved in the implementation of any recommendations and your assignment has been strategic, you should care about the client's journey ahead. You cannot guarantee that clients will act on your next steps plan, but the success of any engagement is based in part on the impact on the client. An assignment with little or no impact cannot be regarded as a success.

Be Clear on the Value-Add that has been Delivered

The ability to create value-add differentiates consultancies and consultants from competitors and individual contractors. A consultant who not only delivers what they agreed to do but also delivers something additional (of value), will be viewed favourably by the client. If any additional value over the contractual agreement has been delivered, attention should be drawn to it to fortify, in the client's mind, the benefits of working with the consultant. Consider drawing attention to any value-add in the following categories: education of the client or client's employees, additional scope delivered free-of-charge, quick wins, overperformance, and any additional legacy that has been left.

Tie Up any Loose Ends

You need to leave the best possible impression with the client to maximise the success of the assignment and to increase the chances of subsequent work. This includes keeping to all the informal agreements made ("I'll just send this article to you", for instance) as well as the major contracted agreements. Typical loose ends include returning any client assets, ensuring final timesheets and expenses are submitted, delivering final invoices or agreeing a time for delivery, and ensuring any feedback being given or sought is delivered.

Keep in Touch

In the case where there is no further work for this client, your next steps should also include proactively planning for continuing your relationship with the client. If you have delivered successfully, integrated culturally within the client's environment, and have had a positive impact, then you will have undoubtedly developed a strong working relationship. In order to leverage all these successes so you achieve your own goal of growing your business, you need to nurture and develop this relationship in the future. There are a number of ways in which you can increase the chances of maintaining regular contact with your client, after the engagement has finished. You can agree to keep in touch though future meetings and agree a specific time to meet in the future, offer to perform a review and follow up on the change at a later period, or perhaps agree to continue to send the client information that they might find useful in the future.

Client Offboarding

As the very final step in the Act stage, you offboard the client from their engagement with you. You move them off your immediate working portfolio. This brings a neat end to your work and ensures that you have the capacity and capability to start another engagement. Each time you offboard, you are attempting to increase your value for future engagements by measuring and learning so that you become more effective and more skilful as you complete each engagement.

Recording Achievement

By recording both your personal and professional achievements, you are building your profile. This in turn leads to a number of benefits, evidence of your capability, and overall improved consulting credentials, which will lead to further opportunities and increased likelihood of converting those into paid business. Remember to consider all of the following: collecting or updating your skills if you have a skills profile, updating your CV or profile, updating your LinkedIn or other social media profile, and documenting a formal or informal case study or providing a social media update.

Measure Personal Success

During delivery breakdown, you will have collected and summarised the outcome of the engagement to the client on two key axes – the delivery outcome and the value realisation. But as you went into the engagement, you also had your own needs and requirements that you wanted to achieve. At the very end of the engagement, it pays to spend some time on these personal elements. You may want to undertake a personal retrospective covering the following three areas:

- **Personal performance.** Did you match the values and the culture of the client, and did you perform to the best of your abilities? Feedback from your client should be sought and listened to.

- **Impact on the client.** Did your intervention result in meaningful change that will be effective in the longer term, not just when you are present?

- **Business growth.** Did the assignment have a positive effect on your business? Did your reputation or capability increase, or did you procure further business, either with the existing client or elsewhere?

Knowledge Collection

Store any deliverables for future reference or future use to constantly build your unique intellectual property. This practice leads to a number of benefits, including content to help you market, which allow you to become more efficient for future deliveries. This knowledge collection should include:

- Client documents, providing these are not covered by IP considerations.

- Generalised or desensitised documents and processes where IP considerations preclude you from using material provided to the client.

- Your personal lessons learned, useful notes, tips, and tricks that you should store and reuse.

- A client engagement summary – a document that records at high level, the requirements, actions, achievements, and technologies of the assignment.

Moving to the Next Engagement

The life of a consultant is very much a cycle of moving from one engagement to the next. As financial achievement (however you measure this) is vital to your success as a consultant, you will continually need to think about the next paid assignment. This is the case even when you are deep in client delivery activities. Without this continual focus, you risk finishing an engagement without having something else lined up. This may be acceptable for a period, or it may simply be poor personal organisation which leads to unrecoverable loss of time.

If you have been keeping up with your marketing and sales activities, or you have been providing effective client management and building relationships, then there is every chance that your next assignment will be lined up before the end of your current one. A controlled and managed end to the engagement is therefore important not only for your current client but also for your next one. It allows you to put all the necessary focus into making your next step a success.

A number of things can happen at the end of an engagement. You may:

- **Continue with the current client.** You immediately move into further consultancy work at the same client, which has been identified and agreed during the previous assignment.

- **Move to the next engagement with another client.** In this situation, there may be no further immediate work at the current client or there may be, and you choose to deliver to a different client anyway.

- **Search for new business.** You have no immediate engagement to move to and you need to generate leads or manage other opportunities.

If you are faced with only one of these scenarios, assuming everything is in place and acceptable to both parties, your choice is likely to be simple. However, the more successful you are, the more in-demand you are likely to be, and the more options will present themselves. If you are presented with a set of options, there are a number of considerations in deciding how to move forward:

- Can you plan to do one and then another? Sometimes this is simple, and you can continue to juggle multiple assignments over a long period by means of careful planning.

- It might not be possible to create a plan where everyone gets what they have asked for. You might need to say no to individuals, but in doing so, do you prevent yourself from winning the work and possibly, all the work that comes after it, or even any other work for that client?

- If you do have to make such a choice, who takes priority amongst the completing requestors? The current client? The highest value client? Do you prioritise the first client who can sign the contract, or the one who you have been courting for a long time and is one of your strategic targets? In truth, there are no easy answers, and all of this is situation dependent. The best that you can deliver at times is open and early communication to everyone, so that expectations are managed.

If you cannot prioritise without significant detriment, then there are other options:

- You could choose to try to perform both roles simultaneously. This may be possible, depending on many factors, including the work types, the deadlines, and the agreements with your clients.

- You could offer a substitute, perhaps another consultant or someone from a partner organisation. In this case, you are handing over the engagement (and perhaps the relationship to someone else).

- You could subcontract, where you maintain the management of the engagement but someone else does the delivery.

- You could augment your business by moving from a sole consultant proposition to a small consultancy. This would require setting up a business, hiring people, and managing employees. This is what many consultants actually do, though it is not a short-term move, and it requires considerable thought before making the leap.

Key Practice 3 – Customer Service

Anecdotally, it takes five to ten times as much effort to get a new customer than to keep an old one. It stands to reason therefore that significant focus should be directed to maintaining your current customer base, and consequently, customer service is paramount.

Customer Service is the interaction of consultant and client before, during, and after the engagement. Good customer service comes from thoroughly understanding your customer's desires, fears, and hopes, including responding in a way that demonstrates they come first. Great customer service comes from going above and beyond in ways that cannot go unnoticed.

A Note on Customer Experience

Customer Experience takes the concept of customer service further, expanding it to include any interaction of customer and brand at any time, whether direct or indirect. For consultants, this encompasses all aspects of your offering, not only your client management and client interactions, but also branding, marketing, content, sales, and referrals, as well as how these elements interact and whether experience is consistent. These touchpoints are all part of what is called the "customer corridor".

A consultant should therefore think about how to provide great customer service during the direct interactions, as well as how the client perceives their overall experience with the consultant throughout the customer corridor.

The Importance of Customer Service in Building Trust

Trust is the belief that another party will act in a way that is supportive and in line with the first party's interests. When a client trusts you, they will:

• Be more open to communicating with you.

• Be more likely to agree to work with you.

• Forgive mistakes or lapses more readily.

David Maister et al., in their book *The Trusted Advisor*,[9] outlined how the amount of trust between two parties can be calculated by looking at four facets of the client–consultant relationship. These four components are as follows:

• **Credibility.** In an earlier chapter we referred to the importance not only of developing capability but also of demonstrating this. Credibility is another way of referring to demonstrated capability. It includes expertise, experience, and how all of this is viewed by others. It therefore includes both rational and emotional elements. Your reputation is also intrinsically linked with your credibility.

---

[9]   Maister, D. H., Green, C. H., & Galford, R. M. (2000). *The Trusted Advisor*. Simon and Schuster: The Free Press. p. 69.

- **Reliability.** If you are behaving positively, consistently, and in a way that the client expects, then you are likely to be perceived as reliable. In addition, your reliability will be more highly rated if contact has been regular. It follows then that you can proactively increase your reliability by finding regular opportunities for a positive contact experience.

- **Intimacy.** To be able to raise and deal with difficult issues with a client, you need to develop a level of intimacy with the client. Developing intimacy is a pattern of offering up a vulnerable piece of yourself and seeing if the other party responds. This means one party inevitably takes a level of risk until the other has either responded in kind, in which case intimacy is increased, or they draw a line.

- **Self-orientation.** If self-orientation is too high, if you are too concerned with yourself or what you have done, and if you tend to explain your solutions before having heard the client fully, then you will damage trust. If on the other hand, you can listen, really focus on the other person, and truly have their interests ranked as a top priority, then you will increase trust. Talk to clients as if they are your friends and you are responsible for their wellbeing.

These facets are interrelated and can be expressed in the following equation – a mathematical representation of the components that make up trust and the relationship between them:

$$T \text{ (Trust)} = \frac{C \text{ (Credibility)} + R \text{ (Reliability)} + I \text{ (Intimacy)}}{S \text{ (Self-Orientation)}}$$

Figure 21. The Trust Equation

This equation indicates that trust increases when credibility, reliability, and intimacy increase, but decreases if self-orientation increases. It also means that you must excel at all three above the line elements of the equation, and that self-orientation has an outsized effect on trust compared to the other elements. In other words, it is difficult to build up trust but easy to remove it.

Customer Service should therefore be focused on the factors that will help build trust. As trust is established, reputation is increased, and business grows. Existing customers will want to do further business with you and will advocate for you. Customers who trust you will provide references, referrals, or case studies and will be amenable to providing you with further information for content and marketing activities, as well as knowledge collection. Conversely, little or no trust results in few or no customers.

Measuring Customer Experience

Whilst all customers are unique, fundamentally they are looking for the same things in any interaction. There are five elements that combine to provide good customer service and a high customer experience. No matter the situation, all customers need you to:

- **Understand them.** To understand what they need, even if they are not able to fully explain it themselves. You also need to help them understand by providing context and explaining details when necessary.

- **Provide them with new ideas.** To make them think, but not to burden them with too much thought. To provide options and possibilities, but never railroading them, always allowing them to make their own informed decisions.

- **Tell the truth.** To give them good news and bad, never telling them what they want to hear. Being caring but not sugar-coating, and challenging them in a helpful and productive manner.

- **Build a relationship.** One that feels real, comfortable, and long term. A good customer relationship goes beyond the transaction and sees the person underneath. And that goes both ways.

- **Offer value.** This means from the relationship, not just the engagement. Good customer service is value outside the transaction, through non-tangible benefits, such as information or support, not just bottom-line benefits and dollar return.

It is possible to take the concept one step further. By converting the principles into a table and marking each client against each principle, you can create your own customer experience score. This can be used to identify deficiencies and strengths and mark progress over time. To get the most accurate picture, you need 360-degree feedback from a range of client stakeholders in addition to your own viewpoint.

	Understand	Ideas	Truth	Relationships	Value
Customer 1					
Customer 2					
....					

Two Models for Communicating with Customers

Whilst customers have equivalent fundamental needs, every customer also has individual needs and must be communicated to and approached in an individual fashion. You should focus on them as an individual, not a role, and target your communications.

The first useful model for targeted communications, which is particularly effective for proposals, is suggested by Robert Miller and Gary Williams.[10] They conducted research on a group of executives and found that they were categorised into five different decision-making styles. These are:

- **Charismatics,** who are initially enthusiastic but have learned to temper this and wait for sufficient information in order to make a final decision.

- **Thinkers,** who slowly and methodically work through data to come to a decision.

- **Sceptics,** who are difficult to convince if something does not fit their existing world view.

- **Followers,** who do not particularly like to rock the boat and make decisions based on how they think others think, or by referencing similar decisions in the past.

- **Controllers,** who focus on facts and analysis because of their fears and uncertainties.

By recognising each type, you can focus your communication in a way that is most likely to appeal to the recipient.

---

[10] Miller, R. B., & Williams, G. A., with Hayashi, A. M. (2004). *5 Paths to Persuasion: The art of selling your message*. Warner Business Books.

The second model is the communication style model. This is based on the premise that all customers (and others, for that matter) understand and learn best when information is presented in a way that meets their preferences. The communication style model guides us to recognise people's preferences and then communicate in a way that each of the four styles find most comfortable. These are as follows:

- **Analyticals** require large amounts of data and information as well as time to digest.
- **Amiables** need to understand the impact on people.
- **Drivers** require short, to-the-point information.
- **Expressives** need to have time to digest and discuss ideas.

In addition, some people are readers whilst others are listeners. Through practise you will learn to make a judgment on the client's style quite quickly and, if necessary, adapt to their style.

How to Respond to Complaints and Concerns

At some point (though hopefully not at too many points), you will receive some level of negative feedback. This may be justified and the result of a failing of yours, or it may be unjustified, or the problem may be as a result of a combination of factors – some under your control and some not. Irrespective of the cause of the concerns, it pays to take it seriously and respond to in a considered fashion. Problem resolution should be approached as thoroughly as it would when you meet a potential client for the first time.

Any concern or complaint raised is an important health check for the relationship. Not all complaints are the same, some being more serious than others, and the language of the communication is, of course, key to understanding the level of seriousness.

Counterintuitively, a complaint provides an opportunity to improve the relationship and, indeed, a relationship is often better if a complaint has been successfully dealt with than if it had not occurred at all. Positive issue resolution allows a deeper and more fundamental understanding of the two parties' interests, and it may become a valuable shared experience. The following process for responding to concerns is effective because it covers a number of bases. In particular, it provides something for clients across all communication styles (which are covered in a section in Chapter 5 – Abilities).

1 First signal that you are Listening (Amiable).

2 Then ask questions (Analytical).

3 Then signal you are listening again (Amiable and Analytical).

4 Then demonstrate you are taking responsibility (Driver).

5 Then suggest what actions you plan to take (Expressive).

6 Then deliver on what you said you would do (Driver).

7 Then check that everything has been fixed.

You may notice that this process is very similar to the consulting process itself. This means that, as a consultant, you are actually likely to be very effective at dealing with issues and complaints because this is a much-practised routine. The difference between complaint handling and needs handling is in the length of the cycle and the importance placed on communication style.

Dealing with Unjustified Complaints

On rare occasions the complaint may be completely unjustified, unfair, vexatious, or even intimidatory and threatening. It is usually wise not to pre-empt this judgement without following through on the process above (though more extreme manifestations are probably clear). However, if having done so, you come to one of the above conclusions, then you are faced with a decision on how to respond and should consider the following:

• Is this in line with previous client behaviour and has this happened before?

• Why do think an unjustified complaint was raised, and what led to it?

• What are your going to do about it – ignore it, raise it, complain yourself, or call a halt to the relationship?

- What is the desired outcome of your proposed action?
- Will your response come out of the blue for the client? Have you acted consistently yourself to this point?

Assuming you wish to act, your action should be self-consistent with how you have behaved until this point. Ignoring the client behaviour will put you on the back foot and make the behaviour more likely in the future. Responding in kind is also likely to lead to difficult conversations in which you lose the moral position you should strive to maintain and have been handed by the client. Instead, it is best to go through an incremental feedback process, which gradually and assertively feeds back the perceived behaviour to the client. This will help you come from a position of strength and consistency, and it means that should the behaviour continue, and you have to pull the plug, there will be no surprises on either side.

Managing Client Expectations

Managing expectations is a key technique in customer service. It helps you align with your customer and avoid future problems, and ultimately, it leads to greater success for both parties. There are a number of ways to make sure that customer expectations are managed so they are realistic and can be met. To effectively manage client expectations, there are a number of steps you need to follow:

- Set a clear scope and confirm the scope once your understanding has increased. This means you should set boundaries on what you will be responsible for and how far you are accountable. Make it clear that you are not there to solve any and every problem that exists.
- Contract strongly with clear terms and conditions. Formal contracts provide the written understanding of the expectations on both sides, as well as the limits.
- Communicate to make sure that everyone has the same understanding. Work out who you need to communicate with and do so in a way that is helpful and informative, though firm.
- Set regular touchpoints and continually communicate to ensure that issues do not come as a surprise. If issues do arise, and you have set

clear expectations prior, then it is also clear whether this is something that you or the client (or both) need to address.

- Insist on what the customer needs to deliver. Make sure the client is clear on their role and the resources and the time that they need to devote.

However, even if you are proactive, there may be occasion when there is mismatch in expectations. In this case it is important to understand which of the following three routes to take:

- If you have set initial expectations correctly and the client is being unreasonable, then push back and do not be afraid to walk.

- If you have set expectations incorrectly and the client is not being unreasonable, then communicate and fix the issue.

- If everybody has learned something new and all expectations need to be adjusted, then the mismatch in expectations must be addressed head-on. But, like any client interaction, it must be addressed helpfully and productively.

Become a Trusted Advisor

Many consultants strive to be a Trusted Advisor. A Trusted Advisor is someone whom the client perceives has reached the pinnacle of the client–consultant relationship spectrum. At this level of relationship, all delivery, and personal and professional relationships are open for dis-cussion, and there is enormous trust between the parties.

"Trusted Advisor" is a term made famous by Maister et al. in their epon-ymous book of the same name.[11] In it, they provide lists of traits that all Trusted Advisors have in common. If all of our dealings with clients are held in compliance with these valuable points, then we are likely to suc-ceed in developing a positive balance of trust over time, cementing the relationship. Here is the list in its entirety:

---

[11] Maister, D. H., Green, C. H., & Galford, R. M. (2000).*The Trusted Advisor*. Simon and Schuster: The Free Press.

Trusted Advisors:

1 Seem to understand us effortlessly, and they like us.

2 Are consistent (we can depend on them).

3 Always help us to see things from fresh perspectives.

4 Do not try to force things on us.

5 Help us think things through.

6 Do not substitute their judgment for ours.

7 Do not panic or get overemotional.

8 Help us think and separate logic from emotion.

9 Criticise and correct us gently, lovingly.

10 Do not pull their punches (we can rely on them for the truth).

11 Are in it for the long haul (the relationship is more important than the current issue).

12 Give us reasoning (to help us think) not just their conclusions.

13 Give us options, increase our understanding of those options, give us their recommendations, and let us choose.

14 Challenge our assumptions (help us uncover the false assumptions we have been working under).

15 Make us feel comfortable and casual personally (but they take the issues seriously).

16 Act like a real person, not someone in a role.

17 Are reliably on our side and always seem to have our interests at heart.

18 Remember everything we ever said (without notes).

19 Are always honourable (they do not gossip about others and trust our values).

20 Help us put our issues in context, often through the use of metaphors, stories, and anecdotes (few problems are completely unique).

21 Have a sense of humour to diffuse (our) tension in tough situations.

22 Are smart (sometimes in a way we are not).

This does not mean that the Trusted Advisor level relationship is the only type that is worth striving for. If a client does not wish to have this type of relationship, then it is perfectly suitable to have a different focus, one based on needs, occasional help through augmentation or simple commercial contracts. Even if they do, you may choose a different route. Perhaps your values do not match. The Trusted Advisor status remains a valuable goal in some circumstances, but not all.

5
ABILITIES

Communication	Problem Solving	Self-Management	Working with Others

Figure 22. The Consultant's Playbook Structure – Abilities

Consultants need expert skills, that is, they need to be experts in the field in which they are providing services. And to constantly remain relevant, you need to keep this expertise up to date. However, there are other skills you must develop in order to succeed in consultancy. These can be grouped into the following broad categories:

- **Communication** skills, that is, speaking, listening, writing, and presenting.

- **Problem-solving** skills, using different types of thinking.

- **Collaboration** skills, including teamwork and influence.

- **Self-management** skills to keep yourself motivated, confident, and productive.

These "soft skills" are a fundamental part of the playbook of the consultant, and you will find yourself using a wide range of these skills over any given assignment. Whilst you do not need to be exceptional across the board, it is important that you work so that you reduce any weaknesses until they are no longer liabilities.

Communication

Communication is the art of understanding and being understood. Good communication occurs when both parties agree that the message being sent is the same as the one being understood. It leaves no room for doubt (though may leave room for further understanding and communication), and leaves both parties satisfied that there is common understanding (if not common ground).

Communication is the number one tool for consultants. Fact-finding sessions, conversations, documents, and presentations are continual, daily activities without which the other expert-focused actions will not succeed. Being able to vary your communication style to suit others, speak and listen effectively, write findings and recommendations effectively, and present to an audience effectively are all fundamental to your success.

Listening

You have a tremendous amount to share – your experience, ideas, and solutions. But in order to gather information to formulate your solutions and to earn the right to speak or to advise in consultancy situations, you need to begin with listening. Most people react very strongly if people do not listen to them, and clients are no different. Listening involves understanding the message, the situation, and the people. In addition, listening is an important part of building relationships – it shows respect to the individual and what they are trying to say. A list of ways in which you can demonstrate effective, active listening, follows:

- Respect the speaker by concentrating on what the speaker is saying (and not what you wish to say next), let them finish and avoid interruptions.

- Look for any underlying messages by checking for meaning, clarifying details, and recognising if your own prejudices are preventing you from hearing the true message.

- Demonstrate you are listening by using body language and recapping from time to time to show you have listened.

Speaking

Having demonstrated that you have listened effectively, you earn the right to put across what you want to add to the conversation. Effective speaking comes naturally to some people but not to others. Speaking is not something that can be considered in isolation; rather, it is integrated with listening, body language, confidence, and situational elements. The art of speaking focuses on content and style as well as these peripheral elements. The rise of collaborative teams has significantly increased the focus on this competency in consulting professionals. The following are important guidelines for speaking:

- Good speakers aim for a confident and regular, clear voice.

- Good speakers use variety and gestures, but too much can distract from the words.

- Warming your voice up can work wonders.

- Big improvements to speech can be made by fixing one or two problems (e.g., omitting filler or empty words such as "basically" and "obviously").

Writing

Great writing is, of course, an art that some people build careers on. The level of writing expected of consultants does not need to attempt these heights, but it should meet a professional standard. Done properly, written material can make a great impression on the recipient, for whom – given the opportunity to understand the message in their own time – ideas take life when presented well on the page. Writing (and rewriting) can also help the writer clarify their thoughts and construct arguments in a way that speech does not allow, thereby leading to deeper personal understanding.

Good writing has a number of characteristics, including being accurate, useful, concise, complete, clear, correct, targeted (relevant), well organised, consistent, and of interest (informative).

Different document types require different styles. An email can be chatty, a recommendations document can be factual, or a piece of marketing may be enthusiastic in tone.

Different audiences require different styles and content based on their communication style and level. The higher up in an organisation your target audience is, the more business focused and succinct; the lower, the more technical and detailed the acceptable style becomes.

Here are ten useful tips for consultants to improve their writing:

1 **Structure your writing.** Bite-size chunks, broken down by theme and headings, make for easier reading and clearer messages.

2 **Signpost.** If people understand where you are going with your messages, they are able to take them in more effectively. An introduction which outlines upcoming sections will help, as will using linking sentences, which show how one point develops from another.

3 **Write as you would speak.** Then tighten up the writing. Using this method, it is easier to write, and it is easier to read what has been written.

4 **Use shorter sentences.** Shorter sentences are usually clearer. But not too short or with many short sentences consecutively, because it delivers a staccato style of writing that makes for an unpleasant reading experience. Conversely, overlong sentences tend to easily confuse and frustrate readers.

5 **Add some variety.** Writing which uses nothing but short sentences may seem robotic and un-human. Occasional longer sentences or a different style of writing helps to hold the reader's interest.

6 **Be natural**, not pompous. Use words you would choose in everyday language and reduce "business speak". If you would feel awkward saying it, it is best not to write it.

7 Write the message then stop. Sometimes a second sentence clarifies and reinforces. Not always, though.

8 Omit unnecessary words. If a word adds nothing to a sentence, it is unnecessary.

9 Tailor your writing to the audience. Your messages should ring bells to keep them interested.

10 Write something unusual. Add something descriptive and memorable to your writing.

Presentation

Presenting is a communication activity that combines all the elements above – writing, listening, and speaking. You will present at key times in your career and usually the outcome matters. You may be pitching for work, presenting solutions to the client, or otherwise demonstrating your expertise.

Chapter 3 – Advise included the Validate step, and in it, a step-by-step presentation approach was discussed. This approach, whilst focusing on delivering recommendations, is valid for all presentation types and can be tailored to suit any level of presentation.

Presentations may differ by length or by content, of course, but you will find over time that the broad structures and headings tend to repeat. The generic presentation structure in the table below can be used to help inform the flow of any presentations you might need to deliver, and you should tailor it to your requirements.

Title	Details
Introduction	A simple introduction may include a history of how the parties were engaged and the format (contents) of the presentation.
Problem Statement	A description of the need that was initially presented, and the true need derived from the analysis activities. The problem statement(s) can also be categorised.

Title	Details
Vision	A vision statement describes the desired long-term results of your client's effort, either for their organisation or simply within the presentation's scope. It can be a single sentence, using clear, concise, and inspiring language.
Executive Summary	A single page summary of the key contents of the presentation, so called because executives (apparently) may be too busy to read the whole presentation.
Key Findings	The most important findings collected as a result of the analysis exercise you have carried out. If more than six key findings are present, you may wish to group the findings into broader headings.
Data and Trend Analysis	If your information is data heavy, you may wish to add specific data (current) and trend (historical) analysis.
Implications	An implications slide provides a projection of what will happen, given the problem and market analysis, should trends continue and no action be taken.
Opportunities	Conversely, by acting there is opportunity, and these potential benefits can be highlighted.
Background	A background slide, which provides context, can include several elements, such as market drivers that have led to this point, or the history of the engagement itself.
Principles	The underlying rules or standards to be applied when considering other elements of the topic.
Plan or Timeline	A high-level view of the stages, steps, or actions, their interaction, and the timeline.
Resourcing	The resources, including people, and equipment needed to implement the plan.
Recommendations	How you recommend that a client proceeds in order to solve their problem.
Solution	The elements of how the identified problem or need can be solved.
Functions and Components	A more detailed presentation may wish to describe how a solution is built up at the lower level.
Next Steps	A recommendation of the next steps to be taken in an effort to gain client agreement to maintain momentum towards positive action.

Title	Details
Return on Investment/ Benefits	A list of qualitative and quantitative benefits from implementing the recommendations and solution.
Market Analysis	Market analysis can be divided into two: information from your own knowledge base and information from external knowledge bases.
Pros and Cons	Advantages and disadvantages of following a certain path.
Options	A single recommendation risks making the client feel disempowered. Providing between three and five options, along with the pros and cons of each, and a recommendation gives the client information and decision-making ability.
Stakeholder Map	A map of stakeholders on a power/interest matrix.
Risks	Key risks with likelihood, impact, and any mitigation identified.

Communication Style

Communication styles differ from person to person. When they are communicating, everyone has a different natural tendency with regard to detail, speed, and focus of the message. When two people with different styles try to interact, the result can range from slight discomfort to mutual bafflement. Understanding the existence of different communication styles is one of the most important things a consultant can learn.

Understanding your communication style and that of the other person makes communication more effective. Firstly, you approach your listening in a different way for each different style; you expect to hear the messages in a distinct way, and when your experience matches this expectation, your listening becomes effective. The experience for the person speaking is much more satisfying since they can communicate in a way that feels comfortable. Conversely, when you are doing the talking it helps to understand how the person you are talking to prefers to receive information. You can then adapt your message in an appropriate way for the listener. This is the same when providing written information.

Of course, when both listener and speaker adapt to the other's style, it provides the best chance of effective communication, as both parties become naturally "tuned" to the other's style. However, when this is not the case, it is usually up to you, as a professional consultant and as the outsider, to change your style rather than expecting the other person to do so. If you happen to come across a client who understands communication styles as well as you, then all the better. There are four types of communicators – **Drivers**, **Expressives**, **Analyticals** and **Amiables**.

Drivers

Drivers are "get-it-done" people. They think and decide fast and need very little information to make their decisions. They are results-focused individuals with good time-management practices. They can be recognised by their serious-looking face, fast speech and movement, louder than normal speech, sparsity of small talk (straight to the point), direct eye-contact, and a focus on tasks.

Expressives

Expressives are strategic thinkers or visionary types. They are outgoing with a significant emotional make-up to their persona. They have significant energy, though time management is a problem for them. They can be recognised by their strong opinions and long explanations of thoughts, scattered thoughts and jumping around in conversation, people-focused conversations, telling it like it is, and energy in interactions.

Analyticals

Analyticals are information and data driven; people whose desire for quality is overriding. They are systematic and well organised and do not take decisions lightly. They are the quietest and most introvert of the styles. They can be recognised by their low-key body language, few facial expressions, relatively quiet volume of speaking, long explanations with lots of information, and indirect rather than direct phrasing.

Amiables

Amiables are "people" people. They are warm and empathetic, often more concerned with other people than themselves. They are great team players and form their opinions slowly. They can be recognised by their tactful opinions, genuine concern in their conversations, range of facial expressions, indirect rather than direct phrasing, and steering away from negative opinions and phrasing.

Problem Solving

Problem solving is in many ways the fundamental reason that consultants like you exist, and it is an activity that you perform, either in full or in part, on a daily basis. In order to make the best decision or determine the best course, you may need to vary the type of thinking you are doing. Understanding this allows you to move between whichever cognitive activities are required at a given point. In turn, this increases your effectiveness as a consultant. Three of the most important thinking types for consultants are analytical thinking, critical thinking, and holistic or systems thinking. The ability to use the right kind of thinking at the right time will lead to effective problem solving.

Analytical Thinking

Analytical thinking involves a methodical step-by-step approach to thinking that allows you to break down complex problems into single and manageable components. It includes gathering relevant information, organising, and categorising it, and identifying key issues related to this information. This type of thinking also requires you to compare sets of data from different sources, identify possible cause and effect patterns, and draw useful conclusions from these data sets to arrive at appropriate solutions.

You may have noticed that this is similar to the consulting process followed in Chapter 3 – Advise. Consulting is very much an analytical activity. In fact, what this indicates is that the solution to many problems can be derived through a consulting process, no matter how it is initially framed. A problem does not have to be introduced as a client issue, need, or requirement to benefit from following the same process.

Critical Thinking

Critical thinking is a cognitive activity where other people's beliefs and statements on an issue are identified and the strength and logic of their positions assessed. The activity is useful for weighing up arguments and reading between the lines so you can draw your own conclusions and establish, as accurately as possible, the truth of the matter. Using the same techniques, you can also analyse and strengthen your own presentations and arguments, which in turn lead to better outcomes and increased influence, with both colleagues and clients.

You will find critical thinking a valuable tool at many points in the consulting lifecycle. For example, reviewing a set of requirements or performing a client interview both require making careful judgements of the information to determine how useful, thorough, consistent, and otherwise valuable it is.

Systems (Holistic) Thinking

Holistic thinking requires an ability to see the big picture, manage multiple inputs and variables, and identify patterns and possible options before using this information to create a solution. It takes into account trends, relationships, and both internal and external interactions.

Understanding how an organisation truly works, how things get done, requires holistic thinking because every organisation of a meaningful size is a product of the individuals, relationships, processes, market, culture, and history that make up and surround the company.

Other Thinking Types

Analytical, critical, and holistic thinking are used almost continually, though there are times when you need to think differently. Here is an additional list with examples of other thinking types that might be necessary to use:

- Supposing you have come up with a new process or tool, you might have ideas as to how it could be used in a new situation. Putting two things together for a new use is a type of thinking called **creative.**

- In addition, it requires you to take the information and understand possible outcomes in situations not yet observed. This type of thinking is **abstract.**

- How about creating a customer process? This requires processing information and creating instructions in a sequential fashion, completing one step before moving to the next. This type of thinking is **sequential.**

- Next, think about having to analyse the output of a report. The information you require is mostly right in front of you. It requires methodically dealing with each output presented and assessing it. This type of thinking is **concrete.**

- Suppose that you have been asked to recommend a new method for increasing sales. Here you have a problem with multiple possible solutions. This requires working outwards from a central point, generating multiple possibilities. This type of thinking is **divergent.**

- How about creating a presentation to summarise the work you and your team have done? This requires the ability to take multiple factors and pieces of information and put them into a logical structure to find an answer or make a recommendation. This type of thinking is **convergent.**

Reframing Problems

Whilst the thinking types above form a formidable toolkit for a consultant, it is also useful to be aware of and practise other problem-solving methods. A particularly useful one for consultants is problem reframing. Problem reframing is the act of changing how the problem is described. The theory behind this is that the words used, in particular the subject of the problem, force you down an overly narrow way of understanding the issue. The reason why this is relevant is that clients may well have a preconceived idea of what solution might solve the problem and conflate both elements. For example, a problem might be phrased as "the management team are not delivering enough new business this year", which focuses the problem around the management team members. An alternative view might be that "the sales process is not delivering the outcome we want". This provides another frame of reference which may then lead the way to alternative solutions.

Self-Management

Self-Management skills help you get the best out of yourself in the variety of challenging situations that consultancy brings. Good self-management means you perform well on a daily basis, across the length of a full engagement, and throughout your career. Managing yourself well leads to a number of positive states, including being motivated, confident, and resilient.

Adaptability

Many times, you can only broadly predict the type, level, and location of work that comes your way. Even if you have the luxury of choosing your assignments, you need to expect variety and adapt fast to the new environment. Projects come in a variety of sizes and shapes. The ability to hit the ground running and make the most of a short period of time with different clients, without having large periods of time to adapt, is necessary. Consultancy engagements are rarely nine to five, nor is project work always regular in terms of workloads or duration.

Initial statements of work, or job definitions, rarely last the test of time. In many circumstances, they are either adjusted for timeline or for scope. Additionally, some assignments are ill-defined, either purposely or otherwise. Either way, expect that at some point the client will require you to do something different to what you initially agreed.

In these circumstances, an email from the consultant to the client, reflecting their new understanding, is wise. Some diligent consultants will do this as a matter of course a few days into an assignment to manage the situation. However, even for experienced consultants, it is not always possible or desirable to adapt. Here are several situations where it is not possible to say yes immediately, and it may require further discussion with the client:

- When the request is something that you do not have the skills for.
- When the request will prevent you from delivering what you agreed.
- When the request is something that runs counter to previous agreements.
- When the request would not add value.
- When the request would risk your reputation or the reputation of your consultancy.
- When the consultancy management have advised against it.
- When there is an opportunity for someone better qualified within your organisation to do it.
- When the requester is not the decision maker (or is not paying for you).

None of these mean the answer is no, rather that more consideration is needed.

Proactivity

Being proactive is almost an entirely good quality to possess. A consultant who is not proactive is not going to last very long. Having to find your own work, influence and encourage others, and keep to the plans and standards you have set yourself requires a certain amount of continual pressure on yourself. You need initiative to set things in motion and drive to see them through. These behaviours are also important in helping you build relationships and give the client confidence that they have made the right decision in engaging with you.

Resilience

Resilience is the capacity to recover quickly from difficulties and is definitely a necessary attribute for consultants of all levels. Consultancy can be a fulfilling profession with variety and financial reward, but it can also be a high-pressure environment. Projects hit problems and roadblocks;

their nature unfortunately means you have no control over timing, and with multiple clients, you have multiple problems to manage. In addition, clients who spend (and therefore can lose) money, become emotional, which can rub off on others and be detrimental to the environment. On top of it all is the continual moving between different clients, which means lots of change, and change can often trigger stress. Plus, depending on your environment, there may be lots of travel with all of the accompanying problems that brings.

Pressure which is not managed can lead to stress and worse, and clients need confidence that you have things under control, so you need to find a way to activate resilience.

The 21st century saw a significant advance in stress and mental health awareness and techniques that can help with building resilience. Most programmes to reduce stress and increase resilience focus on the following themes:

- Having a regular sleep pattern.
- Moderate exercise, especially walks.
- Eating well.
- Finding and sticking to your own working rhythm.
- Meditation and relaxation techniques.
- Finding a purpose (other than work) or a hobby.
- Spending time with close connections.

Emotional Intelligence

Emotional Intelligence is the ability to understand and monitor your own emotions and understand their effect on you, recognise your emotions and their effects on others, and adapt your behaviour in response to this understanding. Popularised by Daniel Goleman in his book *Emotional Intelligence*,[12] Goleman's model applies well to the world of business. It includes the following five constructs:

---

[12] Goleman, D. (1995). *Emotional Intelligence: Why it can matter more than IQ.* Bantam Books.

- **Self-awareness** – the ability to know one's emotions, strengths, weaknesses, drivers, values, and goals and recognise their impact on others while using gut feelings to guide decisions.
- **Self-regulation** – involves controlling or redirecting one's disruptive emotions and impulses and adapting to changing circumstances.
- **Social skills** – managing relationships to move people in the desired direction.
- **Empathy** – considering other people's feelings, especially when making decisions.
- **Motivation** – being driven to achieve for the sake of achievement.

Goleman states that a range of emotional competencies support the constructs and each of these can be developed through practise.

Confidence

Most people do not come out of their comfort zone on a daily basis in their working life. This is not necessarily a bad thing. Having confidence in your current abilities can allow a great performance within the range of activities that you currently do. However, it is when someone uses this confidence to move into a stretch zone that performance can increase significantly. And being a consultant often puts you into a stretch zone.

Changes in confidence do not happen overnight. Although, by identifying how you feel at any point, you provide a foundation for understanding how your feelings may be affecting your work performance. Additionally, most people can bring examples to mind of when they were feeling confident, buzzing, or high, and how this affected their performance or work. Conversely, negative self-talk can affect your productivity enormously. Being able to identify and quickly adjust this behaviour can help manage stressful situations, which are common in the project world.

THE CONSULTANT'S PLAYBOOK

Working with Others

Consultancy without working alongside others is not consultancy. Consultancy is the interaction of an individual or group with a problem or need, with an individual or group who can help them solve the problem or need. In this context, there are three related but distinct concepts that you should familiarise yourself with and practise. These build on each other and the more senior a consultant you are, the more you need to understand and use all of them:

- **Teamwork.** Working alongside others where everyone has a specific role.
- **Collaboration.** Working in a team whilst getting the best out of one another.
- **Influence.** Using techniques and behaviours to encourage individuals to all move in the same direction.

Teamwork

Teamwork is the common denominator of each of the three styles of working with others. As a team member or leader, you will be responsible for delivery of your own tasks, as will others. Everyone has a joint vision and is aiming at an agreed and understood outcome for the group. In this context, it is useful for you to be aware of the concept of high-performing team as you will either form part of, or be responsible for, leading a team.

The concept of high-performing teams has been around for a long time. You will find many definitions. Most seem to have some or all of the following characteristics:

- It has clear purpose, great focus, and known goals.
- It is bounded and clear in membership.
- Members are diverse in talents/styles and able to challenge one another.
- There is a positive atmosphere, including openness, good communication, and an ability to resolve conflict.
- Members are able to make decisions and are accountable.

By affirming any concept regularly, you can embed it into the culture of the team. As a team member you can affirm teamwork by:

- Making sharing of experience the norm.
- Being helpful.
- Communicating in a way that the other person finds effective.
- Being adaptable.

As a leader, you can affirm the importance of teamwork by:

- Incorporating it into everyday activities.
- Using language that always provides cultural affirmation of its importance.
- Setting expectations for the goal of the team.

Collaboration

Collaboration takes the concept of teamwork a step further and is char-acterised by a focus on the ability to work effectively with others, to bring the best out of teammates, and to form part of a unit where the whole is greater than the sum of the parts. Collaboration requires an under-standing of what you can contribute, how others can help you, and a willingness to subvert personal desires (at least temporarily) to the needs of the group. Consultants at a more senior level find themselves not only leading or being part of a team but also collaborating to improve the outcome for everybody. A consultant will need to collaborate with clients as part of a client team, and with colleagues as part of a consultancy.

A large proportion of any consultant's time is spent working with clients, but you are not a client employee. Your ability to maintain a degree of separation is important to both client and consultancy, irrespective of the length of the agreement or how closely you work. There is a commercial and contractual relationship in place, not an employer–employee one, and an implicit or explicit expectation that you are bringing something to the table which is not available internally. You need to integrate well with the client and there are a number of small steps that can help effective collaboration:

- **Work out the culture.** The culture of each environment will differ from client to client. A consultant needs to understand the client's cultural norms sufficiently to not cause disruption or offence, but not to integrate these to the extent of losing their identity or independence. You need to look out for signs from day one.

- **Use "we' not "I".** Practising "we" rather than "I" in your speech helps you mentally change your focus from yourself to your client team. This can be quite a difficult step to master if you are used to working in an individual-focused environment.

- **Be helpful to clients at all times.** Being helpful is more important than being right. Behaviours which encourage, cajole, and nudge a client into the correct decisions whilst treating the client carefully, are usually far more desirable to a client than what may be perceived as hurtful truth-telling.

- **Being proactive.** Proactivity was earlier identified as a positive self-management attribute for consultants, and this is particularly true when you are acting as part of a client team. Proactivity shows you take ownership of not only your own activities but also those that help other team members, which is the essence of collaboration.

- **Build relationships.** Effective collaboration is made much easier by solid mutual relationships. It requires finding time to take a real interest in people, their viewpoints, and how you relate with them. In the initial stages of a relationship, this requires effort until a comfortable point is reached.

If you are part of a consultancy, the other major part of your time will be spent with your consultancy colleagues. So, whilst you need to integrate within your client, you need to maintain independence. Your ability to balance fee-paying work with development and company work is important to long-term success, and no matter how demanding client work may be on your time, space must be carved out to collaborate with colleagues.

- **Mark out specific time to work on your business.** The intensity of client work can make it all-encompassing, so you are advised to find ways to carve out non-client time during your working week.

- **Be helpful to your colleagues.** If you are someone who responds considerately and helpfully, this enables your colleagues and therefore your company by extension, and it also connects you with them.

- **Watch out for "going native".** Sometimes a consultant starts to identify with the client more than with the consultancy. It often happens if the consultant is on-site for a long time, or if contact with head office is limited. You need to be aware of signs that either you or your colleagues have begun to exhibit symptoms of this syndrome.

- **Add to the culture.** To maintain a sense of consultancy identity and connection, it is important to take part in consultancy events that are arranged. These give you the opportunity to re-acquaint socially and to share ideas and experiences.

Influence

In Chapter 4, in the section on Solutions Delivery, the high-performance concept of using leverage was introduced as behaviour for ensuring delivery success. Using leverage helps to increase your influence on-site. You will find, however, that the concept has a much wider implication throughout all your activities as a consultant.

To refresh, certain things enable you to increase your leverage:

- **Results.** Reliably delivering great results for the client.

- **Knowledge.** Having credibility through developing and demonstrating expertise.

- **Attitude.** Being the type of person who others like to work with by being helpful and cooperative.

- **Empathy.** Understanding and appreciating the problems of others and being available for others to share their concerns.

- **Networks.** Building positive relationships and showing intimacy with others throughout client and consultancy organisations.

- **Inclusion.** Involving others in your decisions, activities, and projects.

- **Detachment.** Having a degree of emotional detachment, and being a person who can view things objectively, can increase your standing.

How can leverage be used by consultants outside delivery activities, and how does this benefit you?

- In order to generate business, you need leads. Leads typically come from relationships, marketing, or another factor, namely reputation. Increased influence has a significant effect on reputation. Therefore, by improving your leverage, you are increasing your influence and in turn, your reputation. As your reputation increases, you generate new business opportunities and grow your pipeline.

- Later, during the sales activity itself, influencing your prospect at key points will result in a more successful sales effort and more business. With greater influence, you will achieve greater sales.

- When providing advice, whether this is formal or informal, such as during the Advise process, greater influence means that your advice will more likely be accepted and acted on.

- If you have significant networks, you can use these to the benefit of your client by introducing these external parties to them. This is a significant value-add for your clients.

- When working with colleagues from your firm or partner organisations, you are able to influence these other parties to achieve your own aims.

As a final note, the importance of trust for a consultant has already been discussed. The key factors in the trust equation (reliability, credibility, intimacy, and self-orientation) are closely related to the leverage factors mentioned above. Leverage and influence increase trust and all the positive effects that follow.

Key Practice 4 – Knowledge Management

The world of technology and projects is fast paced. You need to learn sufficiently to keep up but also to improve yourself against this inflating expectation. It is not just the activity of learning that is important, but the mindset that allows you to understand that you do not know everything and that some person or some event could teach you something new.

The ability to learn from each engagement is necessary for consultants, as are processes to make the best of this learning. Without this you have little to offer other than being an extra pair of hands. It is the fact you have experience, having done something before, that makes you valuable to clients. As part of your methods, you should consider how to continually gather your knowledge, distil it, categorise it, store it, and make it available for reuse. This in turn allows you to make it valuable by creating content, education, marketing, and intellectual property as well as providing your own knowledge base for continual improvement and your own learning. This is Knowledge Management.

Learning on the Job

A consultant should look to consolidate what they have learned during and at the end of each assignment. This may be skills, knowledge or abilities, facts, experience, and opinions. Sometimes this learning can be quickly codified, but other times it may be hard to put in words exactly what has been learned. In this case, it pays to put some time aside to step back and consider. This continual learning adds to the capability of the consultant and over time it becomes your own unique selling point. Learning time can rarely be factored into an engagement and if it is, it is not likely to be chargeable. Consultants, however, become more valuable as they take the learning from every engagement on to the next. Taking material from a client engagement may not be acceptable under the terms of a contract unless you have negotiated this. Though, taking notes or creating your own mind maps on useful information at the end of a working day, is simply sensible. Sensitivity around client-specific information is paramount, but generic learnings are absolutely okay.

To clients, the value of consultancies is the skills and experience that they do not have internally. A consultant, though, often needs to replay and communicate this experience to others in the team and to the client. So not only do you need to understand what you can do, you also need to be able to remember and communicate what you have done in the past. Collecting examples and stories from your own assignments that explain what you experienced and how you dealt with it, is an extremely useful technique. Over time you will develop hundreds of these examples that can be used to communicate how previous problems were solved and requirements met. It pays to collect and store these in a repository and to refresh yourself from time to time.

Clients want you to bring experience of similar projects, organisations, and their industry – experience which may well have been gleaned from a competitor organisation or projects. Although, they are rightly wary of and defensive about having the knowledge that has been gained from within their organisation used later, possibly with their competitors. This paradox can be addressed in a number of ways. For both the client and yourself, it is always important to demonstrate honesty and integrity by never referring to previous clients by name or by any other identifier. You must always take care to desensitise any information you collect. You may also be able to mitigate this with agreements for joint IP in your terms and conditions, that is, the right for both parties to use the tools and methods that are created during the delivery phase.

There are opportunities to learn during every step of the consulting lifecycle:

- **Sales.** During the Sales step you are learning about clients and individuals. It is a good time for you to pick up market intelligence – what's hot in the industry and what's top of mind. You also have an opportunity to learn about yourself through the sales activities as you learn what works for you and what you are good at.

- **Analyse.** During the Analyse step you are collecting client data (which can be anonymised, desensitised, and stored) as well as making further observations of the client and by extension, the client's industry. You are also creating a range of potential solutions that can be reused in subsequent engagements (this is your IP since most solutions you create will be discarded and not form part of a client delivery). Finally, you are learning what solutions and methods of presenting are necessary to get the right outcome for yourself and your client.

- **Solutions delivery.** During the Solutions Delivery step, you are learning how to deal with more difficult situations. You are collecting information on how different clients deliver their projects and what mechanisms, methods, and processes they use. During delivery is the time when you are learning in much more detail about the client's business and the industry's needs and drivers. As delivery is usually the phase which lasts the longest and demands the most attention, this is where structured learning gives the most benefits.

- **End engagement.** During the End step, you can perform a project review or lessons-learned exercise, asking yourself and others what went well and what could have been done better. You can consider writing case studies – these may be named and publishable, or they may be unnamed and for your own use. This is the time to get feedback on your own delivery from clients. Finally, you should collect and store the methods, tools, and techniques that you used in your engagement, taking extreme care with client IP and sensitive data.

Using your Learning

Learning can be satisfying and a worthy goal in its own right. For a consultant, however, learning needs to be used to be useful. There are a number of ways to use your learning in consulting:

- **High-quality delivery.** Continual learning, whether it is through acquiring information, knowledge, or skills, means that you can continue to deliver a high-quality service based around your expertise. You make the most of each assignment, not just for the current client, but through continuous improvements, for clients in every subsequent engagement.

- **Marketing content.** What you have learned provides solid material for a variety of marketing activities. You can demonstrate your expertise through articles or videos or engage in group or one-on-one discussion. This type of education-based marketing fits into a wider model of education-based selling. This concept is about continuous customer education, with a view to allowing the customer to make their own informed decisions, all the while trusting that the customer will make the decision to engage with you.

- **Selling yourself.** This is distinct from marketing, differentiated by its "in the moment" nature. You will often find that your knowledge is a great opportunity to sell yourself, your services, and your value when you are meeting with clients or potential clients. This is not just in the Sales step, but in almost any interaction or moment in the consultant lifecycle.

- **Intellectual property.** IP refers to creating new solutions and products which have value and need to be protected. By doing this you are potentially setting yourself up with a commercial advantage that will enable you to grow your business and profit directly from your knowledge. Rules differ between countries; however, you should consider copyright (where original ideas are written down and published), trademark (protecting words and phrases that represent your brand), and patenting (secret processes or methods used to create something). In addition, you should always ensure your contracts with clients allow for continued IP rights rather than assigning these to the client.

- **Educating others.** A real indicator of your expertise is that you feel sufficiently competent and confident to be able to educate others. In your role as a consultant, there are a variety of ways you can educate others, and it is a great tool that you can use to add to your value proposition. These include:

  - Education as a sales tool. A piece of informal or formal knowledge transfer to a potential client during the sales cycle, can help cement your credibility.

  - Education as something to sell. You can sell advice, mentoring, or training courses as part of your services.

  - Education as an indication of partnership. Providing advice indicates that the relationship has become more than a simple commercial transaction and is a value-add that can be provided.

  - Education as a quick win. During delivery, quick wins can provide confidence and momentum to aid the delivery effort.

  - Training to embed change. Education is a key part of a delivery programme and a key tool to ensure delivery change is embedded.

  - Educating colleagues to raise everyone's capability. Education is not just for clients and training, upskilling is extremely valuable for your colleagues and partners, too.

- **Organisational learning.** If you are part of a wider organisation, then you need to consider how to add to the knowledge of the whole company. By regularly collecting lessons from every engagement and centrally analysing and collecting this information, then re-presenting this in an easily understandable form, it takes your learning from just a personal gain to an organisational gain. Knowledge management is the practice of just this type of activity.

Knowledge Management

Given that your expertise and your skills are your value proposition, it makes sense to have methods to manage all of this knowledge. These methods are relevant at three levels:

- Personal – your own collection of reusable assets and knowledge.
- Organisational – knowledge gathered and shared by your own organisation.
- Client – knowledge and information gathered so it can be used by your client.

Research shows that individuals and organisations typically see Knowledge Management categorised into two general strategies – social and codified.

Social strategies focus on personal interactions and communication between individuals and groups. These are most often used in smaller organisations and are more prevalent at a local level. Examples of social knowledge management are communities of practice.

Codified strategies focus on centralised, organised, collected knowledge that is both accessed and added to by individuals. This type is marked by the use of tools and systems. Larger organisations find codification more reliable, and it is suitable for management of strategic information, not just operational. Indeed, some operational knowledge is difficult to codify.

As organisations grow, there tends to be a shift from one strategy to another. Social strategies become much harder to maintain and codification is needed due to the large amount of information that has to be shared. The dominant strategy tends to change from socialisation to codification.

Whatever the situation, organisations should concentrate on one method primarily, with the other supporting. The strategies are quite different culturally and require different activities – using both equally can lead to doubling up on activities as well as poor implementation of either strategy. This in turn leads to multiple sources of truth and gaps.

Knowledge Repository

When constructing a knowledge repository, you need to consider the topics about which you want to collect information; how you might organise, store, and retrieve it; and the types of knowledge assets you want to collect. This exercise is both specific and general. Specific in that the content is related to your required area of expertise, and general in terms of the types of information that will be collected.

The following table includes 15 headings that together cover all the functions of a consulting business. You can use these or a subset of these to create a structure for the knowledge base:

Functional Areas	Description
Strategy and Approach	Setting direction, vision, and values, and building the plan, targets, and value proposition
Organisation	Functions, levels, positions, roles, and structure
Sales Enablement	Producing and maintaining sales collateral, the sales process, and focusing the organisational sales effort
Marketing and Sales	Marketing, lead, and opportunity management and contracting
People Management	Career models, career process, people development and training
Capability	Baselining capability, creating goals, uplifting, and demonstrating capability
Solutions and Services	Service definitions, client, and corporate solutions

Functional Areas	Description
Human Resources	Talent frameworks, health and safety, employment law, benefits, and performance management
Resourcing	Selecting the right resources for assignment and workforce planning
Client Delivery	Onboarding, offboarding, assignment and delivery excellence
Client Management	Building client relationships, ensuring healthy commercial relationships, growing existing footprints, and managing the client portfolio
Administration	Travel, facilities, and event coordination
Finance	Managing financial health, movement of cash, compliance, and management reporting
Knowledge Management	Learning, education, and knowledge management
Information Technology	Providing operational and capital software, IT infrastructure and security
Management and Leadership	Communication, motivation, risk management, collaboration, governance, and strategy alignment

Knowledge Assets

There is a wide variety of asset types that could be stored. Consultants and consultancies typically come across and make use of the following types, though there is, of course, no limit to the types of assets you may wish to store. Whatever the scope, it is important to categorise and group your material for easy reference:

Asset Types	Description
Processes	Processes describe the steps and activities that are needed to achieve a certain end. There are client-focused processes and consultant-focused processes to consider.
Articles	Other people's articles or knowledge can be very useful and should be stored as and when they are found.
Presentations	Examples of presentations and presentation templates which can be reused.

Asset Types	Description
Templates	A structured document with some details in place to help with repeatability.
Guides and Procedures	Procedures are detailed steps and activities to explain how to do things. Guides tend to be collections of procedures with the aim of making sure people can do what they need to do, and the appropriate control can be exercised to ensure compliance.
Multimedia	Videos, webinars, podcasts, and other media types.
Client Deliverables and Examples	If your terms and conditions allow it, you should store copies of your deliverables. If not allowed, you should consider collecting generic elements, or desensitised versions.
Communication Template	A valuable category of collateral is useful communication templates which can be reused when responding to high risk or complex client situations.
Policies	Policies are frameworks to manage people. They are relevant to HR and people management but are used across many functions.
Case Studies	Case studies describe engagements with clients and highlight the successes. They focus on the benefits and value delivered to the client. These can be named and shared with other clients or unnamed and for primarily your own use.
Marketing Collateral	Brochures, videos, social media posts, campaign material, logos or other branded material that can be used to bring attention to your offering.

Maintaining High-Quality Knowledge Repositories

When considering organisational knowledge, it should be of a high quality. Poor or incorrect knowledge is worse than none, giving you a false sense of security, or at the very least, wasting your time. Quality assurance mechanism should be put in place to ensure knowledge is accurate, up to date, informative, and easy to understand. This should include clear roles and responsibilities for everyone involved in maintaining the knowledge repository, as well as the systems and processes that dictate exactly how knowledge integrity is ensured and maintained.

Owners

Owners are responsible for the information contained in the knowledge repository. It is therefore their responsibility to ensure that the information is thorough, accurate, complete, and above all, useful. They make any final decisions on what knowledge should be allowed, and if there are errors or inconsistencies, they are responsible for resolving these. Owners are typically knowledge experts themselves in the area they own.

Champions

Champions encourage both the procurement and use of knowledge for given areas. They encourage people to become contributors and help deliver on the principle of regular updates for the knowledge repository. There can be many champions for a given area or an individual champion may be appointed across many areas.

Contributors

A contributor is anyone who provides information, data, or knowledge to the repository. The greater the number of contributors, the more complete, helpful, and effective the repository will be. This assumes the knowledge provided is high quality, which is assured first, by the contributors following a known process, and second, by regular audits.

Process

A process is necessary to keep the quality of knowledge high. A knowledge management process has the following steps:

1 Contributor identifies or creates the asset
2 Champion or owner reviews the asset and submits findings for consideration
3 Owner assesses the asset for inclusion into the repository
4 Contributor loads the asset into the repository
5 Owner ensures any necessary compliance of the newly added item

Audit

A regular audit of the repository should be performed. Audits should check for the following five characteristics of high-quality information – accuracy, completeness, consistency, uniqueness, and timeliness. Audits are the responsibility of the owner but can be performed by anyone with an appropriate eye for detail and a relevant checklist.

By having these five elements in place, a self-fulfilling prophecy occurs. The more the system is used, the more knowledge is collected and reused, which in turn raises confidence in the system and it is then used more. Conversely, it is easy to lose confidence in the system should the quality be low.

GLOSSARY

Term	Definition
Account Meeting	A meeting between client and consultant to discuss relationship and value-based topics. It may also include delivery topics.
Account Plan	A document with key information about the client that is used to control and plan your interactions with them.
Advise	A three-step consulting process, covering the Analyse, Design, and Validate steps.
Augmentation	A service provided by consultancies, where the consultancy provides a single individual or a whole team and is characterised by minimal management from the consultancy and maximum by the client.
Balanced Scorecard	A method of translating strategy into key measures over financial, operational, customer, learning, and growth dimensions.
Benefit	The positive outcome of engaging with a consultant, which can be financial, quantitative (measurable), or qualitative (not measurable).
Benefit Map	A model which describes various facets of the benefits of implementing a solution so that people understand "why" a project is being run and allows them to see what is in it for them.
Campaign	A set of marketing activities grouped around a theme.
Capability	The skills, abilities, and knowledge that consultants can bring to their clients.
Capacity	The ability to take on work at the time it is needed.
Case Study	A testimonial. A description of a previous engagement, designed to showcase achievement.

Term	Definition
Challenge	To advocate positions other than the client's current understandings or conclusions.
Change	A project or solution introduced by an organisation to improve how it operates, solve a problem, or meet an opportunity.
Change Control	The process of managing proposed change of scope, timescales, or priorities and assessing the impacts. Then ensuring that all impacted deliverables are properly changed and baselined.
Clarify	A process of establishing further detail regarding the client's situation through activities such as interviews and data collection.
Client	The customer of the consultant – the recipient of the knowledge and skills provided by a consultant.
Client Offboarding	The process of removing the client from your working portfolio by recording achievements, measuring your own personal success in the assignment, and collecting and summarising assignment information for future use.
Client Onboarding	Setting up your own systems and process to help you manage the engagement.
Consultancy	The activity of using knowledge and skills to advise and help others to deliver beneficial change.
Consultant	An individual who adapts to perform multiple roles, using their knowledge and skills to influence or deliver beneficial change.
Consultant Offboarding	A process of leaving the client ecosystem, with the objective of ensuring the best possible experience for the client and a clear end to the engagement.
Consultant Onboarding	Performing necessary activities that align you to the client's ways of working and set up the assignment for success.
Contract	A legal and commercial agreement documenting the key details of the assignment. Sometimes known as the Statement of Work, Services Agreement, or Terms and Conditions.
Contracting (process)	To unambiguously detail, then confirm, the agreement between the parties to proceed; and to provide a risk reduction mechanism for both parties through contractually enforceable means.

Term	Definition
Credentials	The consultant's suitability to take on an assignment as demonstrated by previous experience and track record.
Customer	See Client.
Customer Effort Score (CES)	A metric which quantifies the efforts that customers make to interact with you and your services.
Customer Experience	Any interaction of customer and brand at any time, whether direct or indirect.
Customer Satisfaction Score (CSAT)	A metric that can reflect how a customer perceived a specific action that you took.
Customer Service	The non-commercial interaction of consultant and client before, during, and after the engagement.
Delivery Breakdown	A process activity which ensures products are delivered and value is realised.
Delivery Management	Putting in place processes and systems to manage and deliver against the plan to ensure successful implementation.
Domain	An area of expertise, such as an industry or technology.
Engagement Report	A document provided regularly to the client to highlight delivered value and activities performed.
Expert Consultant	A consultant who provides value based on their expertise in a given specialist area.
External Consultant	A consultant who is external to the organisation in which they deliver services.
Governance	The organisational set-up that helps direct and control the actions and affairs of management and others, ensuring that everyone does the right thing.
Industry	The primary business area of a company.
Intellectual Property (IP)	Solutions and products that have value and need to be protected.
Internal Consultant	A consultant who is directly employed by the organisation in which they work to advise and consult, usually on a specific and focused area.
Issue	An actual occurrence of a risk.

Term	Definition
Issue Management	A process including identifying, analysing, managing, monitoring, and reporting issues.
Joint Solution	Involving the client in helping to generate potential solutions.
Knowledge Management	The process of gathering knowledge, distilling it, categorising it, storing it, and making it available for reuse.
Knowledge Repository	Where you store solutions, and commercial or other delivery documents related to the engagement.
KPIs	Key performance indicators – quantifiable measures to judge the success of an organisation or individual.
Lead	An individual or an organisation that might be interested in a consultant's services, but the detail of which is not known.
Leverage (power)	The ability to get things done by using certain techniques to maximise impact.
Leverage (consultancy)	The process of maximising the impact of using senior, experienced consultancy resources as widely as possible by using junior resources to perform tasks which require less experience.
Longlist	A large number of solution options that you later pare back into a shortlist.
Managed Service	The packaging of individual services and management overlay into one overall offering, designed to allow the consultant freedom to deliver and reduce the burden of management on the client.
Marketing	The process of increasing a consultant or consultancy's visibility and that of their services, through targeted and scaled activities, to produce leads.
Marketplace	A panel of consultants or consultancies who present their services in a centralised portal.
Mission	Fundamental aspects of what a consultant wishes to achieve by providing their services.
Net Promoter Score (NPS)	A measurement of all customer loyalty, expressed as a number between negative 100 and positive 100.
Opportunity	A lead with a reasonable potential of becoming a client.
Options	A list of alternative solutions to meet a client need.

Term	Definition
Organisational Learning	An organisational mindset that prioritises the importance of continuous learning for the benefit of the whole organisation. It is closely related to knowledge management.
Panel	A group of suppliers who provide services to a client.
Partnership	An informal term describing a working relationship where a client and consultancy work together for the mutual benefit of both.
Planning	The process of defining tasks to be completed, who will deliver them, their target dates, and the outcomes sought.
Process Consultant	A consultant who generates client-led solutions rather than consultant- or expert-led solutions, with key competencies being problem solving and collaboration skills, and knowledge of organisational behaviour.
Professional Services Provider	An organisation which offers knowledge-based services to clients.
Proposal	A document that contains the solution or service that fits the client's need.
Purpose	A statement expressing why a consultant is providing consulting services. This purpose provides direction to all subsequent activities within the strategy and beyond.
Qualification	The process of understanding whether the consultant or consultancy is capable of and willing to provide a solution.
Qualitative Benefit	Outcome of a service which has value but is less easy to measure financially.
Quantitative Benefit	A hard currency or other numerical amount being attributed to the value proposition or outcome of a service.
Quick Wins	Interim or peripheral deliverables, which provide immediate benefits.
Reference	Reviews from previous clients, case studies, or other external mentions that communicate capability.
Reporting	Communication on progress against predicted measurements or targets, or other consolidated data, to provide information on which project control decisions are made.

Term	Definition
Return On Investment (ROI)	A simple way of showing the effectiveness of an investment by comparing how much cost and how much return will be achieved at defined points over a period.
Risk	The possibility of an occurrence that will affect solutions delivery or outcome, usually with a negative consequence.
Risk Management	A process including identifying, analysing, managing, monitoring, and reporting risk.
Sales	The act of making contact and communicating with potential clients so that they might consider doing business with you.
Services	What you deliver as a consultant.
Shortlist	A limited set of solution options – not too many as to make it too difficult to decide.
Sign Off	Agreement to go forward with the contractual document and the process of applying signatures from both consultant and client.
Skills	Competencies, knowledge, abilities, or expertise used by consultants and organisations.
Skills Matrix	A tool used to collect and rate an individual's set of skills, broken down by category, and scored using a simple scale such as 1 to 5.
Solution	The specific and tailored matching of a service with a need.
Solutions Delivery	The process of implementation of the deliverables through which value will be realised.
Stakeholder Management	The process of identifying and managing people who are affected in some way by the project being delivered, then putting in place activities that ensure these stakeholders act so as to help rather than hinder the successful implementation.
Stakeholder Mapping	The process of understanding the importance of stakeholders before you start the process of managing them.
Statement of Work	The legal agreement (contract) with all the terms and conditions included within.
Strategic Activities	Individual task that together deliver the strategic plan.

Term	Definition
Strategic Plan	A document that includes the key topics that all consultants need to consider, and which contains all the planning and thought done during the two phases: setting the direction and aligning the plan.
Strategy	A set of choices that, when brought together, provide the direction for the future actions, with the aim of increasing the likelihood of success.
Supplier	An individual or organisation who supplies good or services to a client organisation.
Technology System	An information technology system with a unifying theme
Terms and Conditions	The contractual details of an assignment, including working hours, payment terms, terminations, IP and confidentiality, and dispute processes, amongst other things.
Trust	The belief that another party will act in a way that is supportive and in line with the first party's interests.
Trust Equation	An equation that explains how trust between client and consultant is based on the factors of reliability, credibility, intimacy, and self-orientation.
Trusted Advisor	Someone who the client perceives has reached the pinnacle of the client–consultant relationship spectrum.
Value	Overall benefit that a client enables by engaging with a consultant.
Value-Add	The concept of providing additional benefits for no additional cost.
Value Proposition	A way of expressing capability which demonstrates clear benefits of the services provided.
Values	An individual or organisation's fundamental beliefs on how to behave in the business environment.
Vendor	See Supplier.
Vision	A statement that describes the desired long-term results of the consultant's efforts. It is a single sentence (or possibly two), using clear, concise, and inspiring language.

FURTHER READING

The Practice of Consulting

Business Consulting: A Guide to how it works and how to make it work (The Economist Series). Gilbert Toppin, Joe Moran, & Fiona Czerniawska. 2005. Economist Books via various publishers.

Flawless Consulting: A guide to getting your expertise used. Peter Block. 2011, 3rd edition. Pfeiffer: John Wiley & Sons. First published in 1981.

Management Consultancy. Joe O'Mahoney & Calvert Markham. 2013, 2nd edition. Oxford University Press.

Million Dollar Consulting: The professional's guide to growing a practice. Alan Weiss. 2022, 6th edition. McGraw-Hill. First published in 1992.

The Management Consultant: Mastering the art of consultancy. Richard Newton. 2019, 2nd edition. Pearson Education Ltd: FT Publishing. First published in 2010.

The Practice of Professional Consulting: The journey of the trusted consultant. Edward G. Verlander. 2012. Pfeiffer: John Wiley & Sons.

The Seven Cs of Consulting: The definitive guide to the consulting process. Mick Cope. 2010, 3rd edition. Pearson Education Ltd: FT Publishing. First published in 2000.

The Trusted Advisor. David H. Maister, Charles H. Green, & Robert M. Galford. 2021, 20th anniversary edition. Simon & Schuster: Free Press. First published in 2000.

Managing Consulting Firms

How Clients Buy: A practical guide to business development for consulting and professional services. Tom McMakin & Doug Fletcher. 2018. John Wiley & Sons.

Managing the Professional Services Firm. David H. Maister. 2003, 2nd edition. Simon & Schuster: Free Press. First published in 1993.

The Art of Managing Professional Services: Insights from leaders of the world's top firms. Maureen Broderick. 2010. Pearson Education Ltd: FT Publishing.

The Boutique: How to start, scale and sell a professional services firm. Greg Alexander. 2020. Advantage.

Leadership

Good Boss, Bad Boss: How to be the best ... and learn from the worst. Robert I. Sutton. 2012. Hachette Book Group: Business Plus. First published in 2010.

Lead Your Boss: The subtle art of managing up. John Baldoni. 2009. AMAZON.

Sales Management. Simplified: The straight truth about getting exceptional results from your sales team. Mike Weinberg. 2015. AMAZON.

The 360 Degree Leader: Developing your influence from anywhere in the organization. John C. Maxwell. 2011. HarperCollins Leadership. First published in 2005 by Thomas Nelson, Inc.

ABOUT THE AUTHOR

Originally from Leeds in the United Kingdom, Dan was previously Executive General Manager of People Experience and Strategy at Planit Software Testing, one of the top-three pure play quality assurance companies in the world. His specialism is scaling professional services firms' business activities and operations effectively whilst focusing on people experience and career management.

Dan has a BA Honours from the University of Lancaster, and an MSc in Information Technology from the University of Aston. After working in the UK insurance domain, he moved in to work in consultancy, specialising in testing IT systems. Since 2004, he has worked across numerous clients and companies in the United Kingdom, the United Arab Emirates, New Zealand, and Australia. Dan has worked for boutique and large consultancies in the quality assurance and technology sectors, including IS Integration, AppLabs, Certeco, and Planit Testing. Over this time, he has been accountable for the relationships with and successful delivery to hundreds of clients, and responsible for the careers and growth of more than a thousand consultants.

Dan is an avid Leeds Rugby League fan, a lifelong learner, and a history buff. He is married with two children. Dan and his family are based in Auckland, New Zealand.

For further details on Dan
and his work you can visit *danminkin.com*
or connect with him on LinkedIn,
at *https://www.linkedin.com/in/dan-minkin-bb99b214/*

CPSIA information can be obtained
at www.ICGtesting.com
Printed in the USA
BVHW051947060223
657986BV00011B/115